Social Science to Improve Fuels Management: A Synthesis of Research on Collaboration

Wildland Fire Behavior & Forest Structure

Environmental Consequences

Economics

Social Concerns

Preface

This document is part of the Fuels Planning: Science Synthesis and Integration Project, a pilot project initiated by the USDA Forest Service to respond to the need for tools and information useful for planning site-specific fuel (vegetation) treatment projects. The information addresses fuel and forest conditions of the dry inland forests of the Western United States: those dominated by ponderosa pine, Douglas-fir, dry grand fir/white fir, and dry lodgepole pine potential vegetation types. Information was developed primarily for application at the stand level and is intended to be useful within this forest type regardless of ownership. Portions of the information also will be directly applicable to the pinyon pine/juniper potential vegetation types. Many of the concepts and tools developed by the project may be useful for planning fuel projects in other forest types. In particular, many of the social science findings would have direct applicability to fuel planning activities for forests throughout the United States. As is the case in the use of all models and information developed for specific purposes, our tools should be used with a full understanding of their limitations and applicability.

The science team, although organized functionally, worked hard at integrating the approaches, analyses, and tools. It is the collective effort of the team members that provides the depth and understanding of the work. The science team leadership included Deputy Science Team Leader Sarah McCaffrey (USDA FS, North Central Research Station); forest structure and fire behavior—Dave Peterson and Morris Johnson (USDA FS, Pacific Northwest Research Station); environmental consequences—Elaine Kennedy-Sutherland and Anne Black (USDA FS, Rocky Mountain Research Station); economic uses of materials—Jamie Barbour and Roger Fight (USDA FS, Pacific Northwest Research Station); public attitudes and beliefs—Pamela Jakes and Susan Barro (USDA FS, North Central Research Station); and technology transfer—John Szymoniak, (USDA FS, Pacific Southwest Research Station).

This project would not have been possible without the vision and financial support of Washington Office Fire and Aviation Management individuals, Janet Anderson and Leslie Sekavec.

Russell T. Graham
USDA FS, Rocky Mountain Research Station
Science Team Leader

Welcome

This is one of several publications to be developed by the public attitudes and beliefs team of the Fuels Planning: Science Synthesis and Integration Project. To gather information relevant to public attitudes and beliefs about fuels planning, we posed six questions. These questions were developed around the tasks and challenges faced by fuels treatment planners:

- What information and tools are available to help land managers and communities collaborate in developing fuel treatment programs?
- What information and tools are available to help managers work with communities to communicate the risk and uncertainty of fuels treatment projects?
- What information and tools are available to evaluate the social acceptability of fuels treatments?
- What information and tools are available to describe and evaluate the aesthetic impacts of fuels treatments?
- What information and tools are available to encourage more active involvement of private property owners in the fuels management process?
- What information and tools are available to help us understand and evaluate the social impacts of wildfire?

Teams of scientists from universities and public agencies across the country were formed to address each question. Each team had approximately eight weeks to produce a synthesis of science relevant to its question and an annotated bibliography that supports the synthesis.

While the focus of the national project was on the dry inland forests of the Western United States, the research synthesized by the social science teams was not limited geographically. We felt the research question being addressed was more important than the location of the research. In addition, we felt that research addressing the human dimensions of a variety of management objectives is potentially applicable to fuels management. For example, we assumed that information and tools developed in Minnesota to bring together communities and agencies in addressing watershed management collaboratively, across boundaries, are applicable to fuels management.

In this publication we present the findings of the synthesis on collaboration. An annotated bibliography and a series of manager fact sheets have been prepared to accompany this synthesis. Manager fact sheets are available online at: http://www.fs.fed.us/fire/tech_transfer/synthesis/social_science_team/fact_sheet_ss.htm

Further information on the larger project is available online at:
http://www.fs.fed.us/fire/tech_transfer/synthesis/synthesis_index

Social Science Leaders: Pamela Jakes   Susan Barro

(651) 649-5163   (651) 649-5158

pjakes@fs.fed.us   sbarro@fs.fed.us

Victoria Sturtevant
Institute of Environmental Studies
Southern Oregon University
Ashland, Oregon

Margaret Ann Moote
Ecological Restoration Institute
Northern Arizona University
Flagstaff, Arizona

Pamela Jakes
North Central Research Station
USDA Forest Service
St. Paul, Minnesota

Antony S. Cheng
Department of Forest, Rangeland & Watershed
Stewardship
Colorado State University
Fort Collins, Colorado

Contents

Introduction

Wildland fire professionals at the Federal, State, and local levels have a long tradition of collaboration across agencies and jurisdictions. However, citizens, managers, and policymakers continue to express the need for more and improved collaboration for wildland fire and fuels management. In this synthesis of research on collaboration, we offer knowledge and tools to improve collaboration in the field—at the level where wildland fire and fuels management projects are planned and implemented. This synthesis was commissioned by the United States Department of Agriculture Forest Service (Forest Service) to aid fuels mitigation project planning under the requirements of the National Environmental Policy Act (NEPA). However, collaboration is not an activity that fits neatly into any one stage of the NEPA process or chapter in a NEPA document; rather, it is an ongoing process that is most effective when maintained at every stage of both program and project planning. Collaboration during program planning helps ensure dialogue that can support and improve various NEPA activities such as scoping, defining desired future conditions, identifying purpose and need, developing and evaluating alternatives, and monitoring. Although many of the examples offered in this synthesis involve the Forest Service, the knowledge shared here can be used by communities and citizen groups as well as agencies at local, State, and Federal levels to improve land use planning and management through collaborative action.

"Certainly, fire management and suppression is an area in which collaborative approaches make perfect sense, and in which it makes no sense at all to not collaborate."
(Pipkin and Doerksen 2000, p. 75)

This report is a companion to a managers' report on social science to improve the development and implementation of fuels management projects (in process), but it provides more detail on what social scientist research has discovered about collaboration. Even more information can be found in the studies cited in this synthesis. To help readers locate this information and to identify which publications might be useful in justifying and supporting efforts for wildland fire collaboration, a CD-ROM is enclosed that contains an annotated bibliography of the literature on collaboration relevant to wildland fire and fuels management. This is not an exhaustive bibliography, but it is a good introduction to the abundant scientific literature that addresses collaboration in general, the more limited scientific literature on collaboration for natural resource management, and the very limited scientific literature on collaboration for wildland fire.

Collaboration and Wildland Fire

Collaboration is not a new idea for public land managers. Surveys of national forest employees in the mid-1990s found interest and support for implementing a more collaborative approach to interacting with the public (Mohai *et al.* 1994, Mohai and Jakes 1996). At the time of these studies, some level of collaborative planning was reported on 91 percent of the national forests (Selin *et al.* 1997).

Wildland fire management offers many examples of interagency collaboration, with agencies discovering
"that they could develop better and long-lasting solutions for complex resource problems by working together [rather] than by attempting to deal with the problems on their own" (Pipkin and Doerksen 2000: iii).

Beyond coordinated response to fires, wildland fire professionals have created common training and standards; have shared information, equipment, supplies, and personnel; and, more recently, have collaborated on research, fuel hazard reduction, and public education.

One example of wildland fire collaboration at the national level is the National Interagency Fire Center (NIFC). NIFC was established in 1965 when the Bureau of Land Management (BLM) and the Forest Service joined forces to improve support for firefighting in the West. The Department of Commerce's National Weather Service contributed fire weather forecasting to the NIFC effort, and in the 1970s four more agencies from the U.S. Department of the Interior—the National Park Service, Bureau of Indian Affairs (BIA), Fish and Wildlife Service (FWS), and Office of Aircraft Services (OAS)—joined NIFC (Pipkin and Doerksen 2000).

A second example of wildland fire collaboration at the national level is the National Wildfire Coordinating Group (NWCG). Created in 1976, the NWCG is made up of members of NIFC and the National Association of State Foresters. The goal of the NWCG is to coordinate programs of the participating wildland fire management agencies to improve efficiency and provide a framework for working together (NWCG 2004).

There are numerous examples of wildland fire collaboration at the local level. Local volunteer fire departments share training, equipment, and facilities with partners at the State and Federal level. Community groups and agencies come together in organizations such as local fire councils to collaborate on planning and conducting fuel treatments. Programs such as Firewise, FireFree, and Fire Safe bring together diverse partners to encourage and support wildland fire management activities. Many of these collaborative efforts improve not only the management of wildland fire, but also the overall health of forests and other components of fire-dependent ecosystems (Sturtevant and Jakes 2003, Teie and Weatherford 2000, USDA 2003).

Although collaboration in wildland fire management has been significant, calls continue for more collaboration, especially at the local level. In a joint report by then USDA Secretary Dan Glickman and Department of the Interior Secretary Bruce Babbitt to President Clinton after the fires in the summer of 2000, it was suggested that Federal fuels treatment teams work closely with local communities (USDA and USDI 2000). Congress, in its appropriation for the National Fire Plan, directed that there should be "a collaborative structure, with the states and local governments as full partners .... Successful implementation of this program will require close collaboration among citizens and governments at all levels" (USDA and USDI 2001, p. 5).

Recognizing that community engagement can make an initiative more enduring, this report ends by suggesting, "Key decisions should be made at local levels."

In a report to the NWCG, managers and the public identified critical social science research questions for wildland fire management (Machlis *et al*. 2002). The number one question emerging was "How can Federal agencies best share responsibility for fire management with non-Federal landowners?" A study by the National Academy for Public Administration points to the added difficulty and costs of fighting wildland fires due to the growth of the "wildland-human interface," and suggests that collaborative efforts are needed for addressing the growing risks of wildland fire (NAPA 2003).

More recently, a handbook for implementing the Healthy Forests Restoration Act of 2003 (HFRA) emphasizes the importance of communities and Federal agencies working together to develop projects to reduce hazardous fuels (Society of American Foresters 2004). As a requirement for funding, communities must develop community wildfire protection plans that are developed collaboratively with government representatives from local and State levels, and in consultation with Federal agencies and other interested parties. The HFRA clearly recognizes that wildfire and fuels management is no longer solely the responsibility of Federal agencies, but is rather a shared responsibility. Collaboration is as crucial as ever in meeting this responsibility.

What follows is a synthesis of published research relating to collaboration and relevant to wildland fire and fuels management. The synthesis is organized in topics as follows:
• Definition of collaboration
• Benefits of collaboration
• Stages of collaboration
• Challenges for building and sustaining collaboration
• Policy resources for collaboration
• Keys to successful collaboration

Definition of Collaboration

Collaboration is the "pooling of appreciations and/or tangible resources, such as information, money, labor, etc., by two or more stakeholders to solve a set of problems which neither can solve individually" (Gray 1985, p. 912). Although there are many definitions of collaboration, most collaborative relationships are (1) voluntary, (2) involve face-to-face interaction and interdependence, and (3) seek to achieve specific goals (Wondolleck and Yaffee 2000). In general, collaboration helps people achieve goals together that they could not achieve independently (table 1). Some people find that they better understand what collaboration is by studying the different types of groups that may be labeled collaborative. Readers can find a detailed discussion of the types of collaboration in appendix A.

Table 1.—Characteristics of Collaboration *(BLM and Sonoran Institute 2000, NWCG 1999, USDA 2000, USDI 2000)*

Collaboration is...	Collaboration is not...
... a means of achieving a goal.	... a goal in and of itself.
... a process that has been around for centuries.	... new.
... one tool to use in project planning and implementation.	... a silver bullet that will eliminate conflict and controversy.
... a voluntary, mutually beneficial, desired arrangement.	... something that can be forced.
... fair and conducted in good faith.	... a way of manipulating or co-opting groups or interests.
... a complement to public involvement activities.	... a substitute for public involvement.
... a sharing of authority or responsibilities.	... an abdication of authority or responsibilities.
... one approach to wildland fire and resource management.	... always the best approach.

Collaboration in forestry and natural resources often focuses on collaborative stewardship. Collaborative stewardship is defined as:

- "... voluntary, mutually beneficial, desired arrangement between groups... established to accomplish mutual objectives that are consistent with the mission of each group" (NWCG 1999, p. 10).

- "People working together, sharing knowledge and resources to ensure ecological systems and communities" (USDA 2000, p. 1).

- "A cooperative process in which interested parties, often with widely varied interests, work together to seek solutions with broad support for managing public and other lands" (USDI and Sonoran Institute 2000, p. 3).

- "A cooperative process in which interested parties work face-to-face to resolve a natural resource problem, create a new policy, or develop a management plan" (Cestero 1999, p. 9).

Benefits of Collaboration

Why should project managers collaborate? Because a new law requires it? Because a supervisor tells them they must? As usual, the best answer is the simplest: "Collaboration can lead to better decisions that are more likely to be implemented, and at the same time, better prepare agencies and communities for future challenges"

Table 2.—Benefits of Collaboration for Different Wildland Fire or Fuels Management Issues and Concerns *(TNC 2003)*

Wildland fire or fuels management issues and concerns	Benefits of collaboration
Lack of adequate funding for projects and programs	Collaboration can mobilize people and organizations to generate funding.
Lack of quality, usable data and other resources	Collaboration facilitates the sharing of data, expertise, and data.
Perceived and real resistance and mistrust	Collaboration leads to coalitions and support.
NEPA planning requirements	Collaboration can lead to interagency and community technical teams that facilitate the NEPA process.
Incompatible attitudes towards fire	Collaboration leads to broader understanding of different attitudes and values through outreach and shared learning.
Conflicting project timelines, standards, and objectives	Collaboration can lead to coordination, cooperation, and increased effectiveness and efficiency.

(Wondolleck and Yaffee 2000, p. 23). Below we summarize (table 2) and discuss several benefits of collaboration for those involved in fuels management.

Collaboration Increases Efficiency

Although the responsibilities of natural resource managers have increased in complexity, budgets to fulfill many of these responsibilities have diminished and competition for new dollars has intensified (Pipkin and Doerksen 2000). Even with increased funding for fuels reduction on Federal lands, efficiency is monitored to ensure responsible use of public funds. Collaboration can create agreements that result in increased efficiency through the sharing of personnel and equipment—means to combine resources for mutual benefit (Wondolleck and Yaffee 2000). Collaboration also results in relationships that help agencies and organizations leverage resources by qualifying for grants that provide matching funds (USDA 2000). Collaboration can increase efficiency by mobilizing citizens who provide volunteer labor for projects or help organize and conduct fund-raising activities (Loucks 2002). Greater efficiency is also realized through the sharing of data and analyses. Although collaborating may initially take more time and funding than not collaborating, research has demonstrated long-term benefits including increased efficiency and "bang for the buck." One study reported, "Many respondents noted that collaboration could improve cost-effectiveness at the organizational and interorganizational level" (Imperial and Hennessey 2000, p. 18).

Collaboration Increases Agency Awareness of Changing Values

Social values are changing and becoming more diverse (USDA 2000). Attitudes, values, and beliefs about wildland fire and fuels management are also in flux. Various groups, aided by the "information highway," have increased the range of public interest and understanding of resource issues. Through collaboration—building coalitions, identifying common ground, engaging in collective learning, and sharing information—public land managers can better identify, understand, and respond to these changes (USDI 2000).

Collaboration Builds Trust

It is commonly acknowledged that trust in government, including public land management agencies responsible for wildland fire and fuels management projects, is not what it could be or has been. However, when we talk about trust in government, we need to distinguish between trust in the government agency and trust in the individual government employee. Although local residents may distrust the agency, they tend to trust the individual employee ("I trust the Ranger, just not the Forest Service"). When Federal employees participate in collaborative activities as individuals, trust builds between members and may eventually include the agency (Sturtevant and Lange 2003).

Collaboration is part of a movement to counteract special interest politics and cynicism about government to "reawaken" (Brick 2001) community with a focus on stewardship. By collectively defining fuels management as one step to improving forest health, managers—with the community's support and understanding—can make the case for being responsible stewards of the land. Indeed, in some cases, collaboration seems to be the only process that will work (Brick 2001, Kusel and Adler 2003).

Members of SWIFT work together to create and maintain fuelbreaks across ownerships, accomplishing together what no one agency or group could do alone.

Collaboration Facilitates Landscape-level Management and Planning

Managers are looking across ownership boundaries to promote sustainable resource management at the landscape level (USDA 2000). Although fuels mitigation projects may be planned and implemented at the district or local level, to be effective they must support a broader landscape-level plan for

fuels management. Several case studies of collaborative groups working in watershed restoration describe the positive results of joint resource management planning (Born and Genskow 2000, Brunner *et al.* 2002, Imperial and Hennessey 2000, Porter and Salvesen 1995). Examples include development of joint watershed management plans; resource sharing (e.g., expert from one agency lent to another; interest group collecting data for agency); joint grant proposals; and, in a few cases, the creation of intergovernmental organizations, Federal-State compacts, and shared regulations.

Technical advances support and enhance landscape-level planning across jurisdictional boundaries (Yaffee and Wondolleck 2000). Collaboration facilitates synthesis of information in a manner that "adds value" for decisionmakers, enhances project-level efforts (Imperial and Hennessey 2000) and increases access to information through collaborative-sponsored clearinghouses (Born and Genskow 2000) and forums for discussing technical issues (Steelman and Kunkel 2003). Cooperatives such as the Southern Sierra Geographic Information Cooperative are working to provide Web sites with software and data downloads for coordinated watershed and fire planning (Birkholz and Lineback 2001).

Collaboration Motivates Private Landowners

One of the major challenges facing those involved in wildland fire and fuels management is motivating individuals to take responsibility for the necessary activities on their land. Landscape-level forest health needs such as fuels mitigation demand landscape-level, multi-ownership solutions. Watershed council projects are often held up as models of projects that work across ownership boundaries and engage private citizens. Although involvement of private landowners in watershed groups is uneven (Waage 2003), studies of wildland fire and fuels management planning show that collaborative projects have promoted personal responsibility and motivated landowners to mitigate their own, as well as their

Photo credit: Victoria Sturtevant

Collaboration involves private landowners helping to define objectives and prioritize projects.

neighbors', vulnerability to fire (Firewise Communities/USA 2003, Steelman and Kunkel 2003, Sturtevant and Corson 2003). However, to be motivated individuals must understand the problem being faced:

> Only when the public truly understands the nature of the wildland/urban interface fire problem will the community-based coalitions needed to effectively mitigate the problem be successful (Teie and Weatherford 2000, p. 29).

Collaboration Supports Science

Scientific "truth" is being debated more publicly and contentiously than at any time during the last century. Non-agency scientists have grown in number (USDI 2000); and independent scientists, agency retirees, and university scientists have entered the "my science, your science" or "dueling scientists" contests. Collaboration among agency, university, and community scientists can facilitate a move to "our science" and "civic science," a "gyroscope" for the conflicting information and values (Lee 1993). A shift is occurring away from the agency as "expert" toward shared learning and responsibility (BLM and Sonoran Institute 2000). Residents bring their knowledge and skills to planning, implementation, and monitoring of projects, as in the participatory mapping project that created GIS data layers for the Trinity County Fire Safe Council (Everett in press). Application of local knowledge and site-specific skills can anchor projects in the place, meshing science with local knowledge (Loucks 2002).

Collaboration Produces Intangible Benefits

Many of the benefits of collaboration are intangible, or what have been called "invisible successes" (Korfmacher 1998). New attitudes, shared knowledge, support, and working relationships can lead to new policies and governmental initiatives that reflect the new perspectives gained through partnership (Moore and Koontz 2003). Other research finds improved job satisfaction and motivation among agency workers as a result of collaborations breaking down political and bureaucratic barriers between agencies (Imperial and Hennessey 2000). Agency managers report that the "greater public support for action" (Born and Genskow 2000) improves their job satisfaction.

Public support broadens the base of political support. Community leaders can advocate for agency projects and policies, assisting in public outreach and serving as "ambassadors" who take the "reduce hazardous fuels" message to neighbors (Sturtevant and Jakes 2003).

Collaboration Builds Community Capacity

Collaborative projects build community capacity, the "ability of residents, community institutions, organizations, and leadership to meet local needs and expectations" (FEMAT 1993, p. vii-51).

Collaborative forest planning, ecological restoration, and education projects have brought people together not only as stewards of public and private land, but also as empowered citizens. As such, citizens may be able to sustain wildfire and fuels management programs into the future on their own, without constant assistance from Federal land managers. Indeed, case studies of collaboration demonstrate an increased sense of civic responsibility and heightened involvement in community affairs (Kusel and Adler 2001). For instance, the shared vision, sense of place, and recognized successes of the Applegate Partnership have translated to other groups in the valley, creating "social capital" and a proliferation of community forums for civic action regarding local economic development and reinvestment, land use zoning, and stewardship of public resources and facilities (Sturtevant and Lange 1995). In turn, this network of community groups facilitated the Applegate Fire Plan process and its fast track schedule for completion. Community capacity will be discussed further in the chapter "Challenges for Building and Sustaining Collaboration."

> *Collaborative forest planning, ecological restoration, and education projects have brought people together not only as stewards of public and private land, but also as empowered citizens.*

Collaboration Builds Agency Capacity

Collaboration can increase the ability of agencies and organizations to meet their missions and goals. Collaboration allows agencies to expand the scale and complexity of projects, expand technical expertise, and garner additional support for activities (TNC 2003). Imperial and Hennessey (2000) found that benefits of collaboration in watershed groups "included doing projects at less cost and undertaking projects that would not otherwise have occurred or would have taken longer to complete without collaboration."

Although it may be difficult to measure ecological benefits of collaboration, researchers have shown that watershed collaboratives have developed important education programs and undertaken activities (constructed sewers, completed habitat restoration projects) that could be expected to improve environmental conditions (Imperial and Hennessey 2000). A study of six collaborative watershed initiatives in three states showed that collaborative environmental management can result in demonstrable environmental progress (Born and Genskow 2000).

When interested agencies and groups participate in collaborative projects, their sense of ownership makes implementation more likely to succeed. It produces "better outcomes for all of us" (Belden *et al.* 2001), a message that can appeal to both self and public interest.

A Summary of the Benefits of Collaboration

We can summarize the benefits of collaboration by looking at what can be gained from the perspectives of agencies, communities, individuals, and society. For agencies, collaboration can improve (NWCG 1999, USDA 2000, USDI and Sonoran Institute 2000):

1. relationships, understanding, and support among agencies, and between agencies and the public,
2. decisions and the ability to get work done,
3. the planning, assessment, and conducting of projects across boundaries and resources,
4. project effectiveness and efficiency,
5. job satisfaction of employees, and
6. opportunities for leveraging funding and enhancing institutional capacity.

For communities, collaboration can (Baker and Kusel 2003, Bernard and Young 1997, Cortner and Moote 1999, Weber 2003):

1. reinforce democratic values and civic culture,
2. build capacity, networks, and relationships,
3. enhance an ethic of stewardship and collective responsibility,
4. connect natural resources to community needs, and
5. create multistakeholder ownership of process, outcomes, and measures of success.

The benefits of collaboration for fuels management can be illustrated with an example. Environmental-group appeals and residents' complacency about the risk of wildland fire presented obstacles for fuel reduction projects proposed by the Santa Fe Municipal Watershed Project (Steelman and Kunkel 2003). To build confidence, a technical advisory group of local scientists was formed to provide third-party review of monitoring and management activities. An all-day technical workshop presented by the collaborative group convinced skeptical environmentalists of the reality of wildland fire risk in the watershed and soundness of their adaptive management approach. The group is also sponsoring workshops and outreach with residents about wildland fire risk and desirability of fuel reduction.

For individuals, collaboration can (Firewise Communities USA 2003, President's Council 1997):

1. advance self-interests,
2. make one's surrounding neighborhood healthier and safer,
3. increase one's ability to define problems and craft solutions,
4. provide access to resources (money, equipment, and technology) for fuel reduction, and
5. facilitate learning about fire risk and mitigation possibilities.

For a society interested in sustainable natural resource management and use, collaboration can (Duane 1997, Dukes and Firehock 2001, Kenney 1999):

1. produce more environmentally sound and ecologically integrated decisions,
2. bring innovative and longer term solutions, and
3. create environmental gains beyond the minimum standards required by laws or policies.

Photo credit: Pamela Jakes

On the Bobar Project in southwestern Oregon, the Bureau of Land Management used stewardship contracting to accomplish a high priority thinning project.

Stages of the Collaborative Process

Outlined below are six dimensions of collaboration usually called "steps" or "stages" (Bentrup 2001, Moote 2003, Pipkin and Doerksen 2000, Round Tables 1998, Selin and Chavez 1995, Sirmon 2001, USDI 2000); movement from one to the next is seldom linear. The context of collaboration, including characteristics of the local geographic community or communities of interest, affects its course. Antecedents—mandates, incentives, or crises (Selin and Chavez 1995)—will affect the speed and urgency of movement from one 'stage' to another.

Initiation: Identifying the Issue and Context

The first task in developing a collaborative process is identifying the problem that needs to be addressed. In identifying the issue, collaboration is given an identity that stakeholders can use in determining and communicating their course of action (Selin and Chavez 1995). Issue identification can be a delicate matter: residents need to be alerted to the danger of wildland fire, but do not respond well to scare tactics; local governments are interested in attracting development and shy away from too many planning regulations. In addition, who defines issues may be as important as what issues are being defined. Having a broad range of interests and experiences represented in this phase is critical. Bringing credible information to the issue, such as maps of fire history or scientific information about fire-dependent ecosystems, may help frame the issue, grounding it in neutral territory.

Successful collaborations begin with issues that are considered to be urgent by the community, but for which there is no clear consensus (Sirmon 2001). A sense of crisis, such as wildfire, provides incentive to cooperate; an outside threat can unify a group otherwise not able to find common ground. From wildland fire the group may move on to broader issues such as ecosystem health, threatened and endangered species habitat, or old-growth management. (Sirmon 2001).

Very early in identifying issues and defining context it is important to assess whether the situation is favorable for a collaborative process. If there is not adequate time and money to initiate the process, if policies and legal restrictions do not allow collaborative decisions, if experienced third-party neutral facilitators are not available, and if levels of conflict are not manageable (i.e., parties are not willing to listen to one another's views), it will be difficult to get meaningful participation or build trust (Linden 2002, Margerum 1999).

Coming Together: Gathering Players

Problem identification will help determine how to gather players, leaders, and "integrators" (Pipkin and Doerksen 2000). The core could be already-cooperating fire agencies—"agencies ... that may be asking the same questions and seeking similar solutions" (NWCG 1999). Interagency fire managers have been galvanized to collaborate (Pipkin and Doerksen 2000), and their coordinated system of fire management can serve as a foundation for wider collaboration with the public. To this core could be added committed citizens, and more partners as the group gains momentum (Sturtevant and Jakes 2003). Agencies are brought into the process for their resources, support, and participation; for example, the State's lead role in cooperating with local fire departments for wildland fire protection (NWCG 1999) would suggest that State departments of forestry or natural resources could join the Federal agencies in initiating wildland fire collaboration. Groups or organizations as yet outside the process may bring additional opportunities and challenges.

Initiating a dialogue about wildfire and fuels management is typically the job of land management agencies. However, agencies are not always effective at convening a sufficiently large, representative, and active group of community stakeholders. At this time it might be helpful to bring in a local convener, someone widely perceived as fair and respected (Moote 2003), who can help bring people together. Care should be taken to ensure that conveners have the skills, funding, and time to conduct the process effectively (Daniels and Walker 2001, Dukes and Firehock 2001, Wondolleck and Yaffee 2000). It may be necessary to seek training for conveners and to educate key participants on collaborative techniques (Daniels and Walker 2001).

Photo credit: Pete Ribble

Deschutes County Project Impact found that partners were critical to the success of its projects.

Trusted community leaders are important partners at the start (Singleton 2002, Wondolleck and Yaffee 2000), and increased communication with public officials may enhance their positive response. (Lowrie and Greenberg 2001). Local "sparkplugs" concerned by the threat of wildland fire in their neighborhoods can help launch the effort (Sturtevant and Corson 2003) and connect the planning process to community networks. Nonprofit and volunteer community groups, an essential part of those networks, will make a substantial difference (NWCG 1999), providing organizational leadership and resources (Sturtevant and Lange 1995). As part of this stage, it is essential to have conversations to clearly define everyone's roles, responsibilities, and expectations for the process and potential outcomes. Unclear roles and unrealistic expectations can doom a collaboration. Table 3 includes a list of potential players in collaborations for wildland fire and fuels management.

Table 3.—Sources of Potential Members for a Wildland Fire and Fuels Management Collaboration

Natural resource agencies	Other public agencies	Communities of place	Communities of interest	Business and industry
• Local (county forestry) • State (forestry, game and fish, parks) • Federal (USDA Forest Service, USDI National Park Service, Bureau of Land Management, Bureau of Indian Affairs, Fish & Wildlife Service)	• County emergency management and planning • County sheriff • State military organizations • County zoning or land use planning	• Elected officials • Tribal leaders • Neighborhood associations • Grange and other voluntary organization leaders • Watershed group or other bioregional group leaders • School administrators University faculty or administration • Other institutions such as churches, hospitals, etc.	• Regional conservation groups • Local conservation groups • User groups • "Friends" groups	• Timber, logging, manufacturing firms • Development • Real estate • Tourism and recreation • Financial institutions

Setting Priorities: Establishing Goals

"Common goals must be the basis for any cooperative project. Think as large as is practical, utilize varied expertise efficiently, and burn together. Opportunities for action will improve as a result."

(TNC 2003, p. 2)

An early step in developing a collaboration is agreeing on goals so that members clearly understand the purpose of their involvement (Ingles *et al.* 1999, Rickenbach and Reed 2002). Goals are created by discovering, and then building, upon the common ground of place or community, or in response to a shared threat. A written mission, vision, or purpose statement will underscore this common purpose, values, beliefs, and goals (Selin and Chavez 1995). It can serve as a reference to keep participants focused during the process, especially when the group is in conflict or considering strategic efforts, and it can reunite the group when motivation and cohesion wane (Sturtevant and Lange 1995).

Creating a "situation map" gets people not only to define issues and goals, but also to discover how they are interrelated. The goal is to get all stakeholders involved in the collaboration to think systemically about the situation rather than focus on linear cause-and-effect relationships (Daniels and Walker 1996, Yaffee *et al.* 2004). This process lays important groundwork for later evaluation and monitoring.

Getting Organized: Creating a Collaborative Structure and Process

The group must agree upon a process structure, including meeting times and formats, working groups, required resources, communication protocols, and other ground rules. A highly trained and experienced facilitator is especially helpful at this stage. The need to reach a broad range of interests should guide the scheduling of public meetings and designing of other methods of outreach. The group should decide how to solicit information from concerned citizens, scientists, and managers at both the local and national levels, thereby supporting a fair representation of broad interests (Blumberg 1999, Singleton 2002). Protocols on attendance, confidentiality, and representation (identifying responsibility to share information with and represent the interests of constituents) may be needed (Round Tables 1998). Little considerations can make a big difference, such as where and when to hold meetings so that rural residents and people who have daytime jobs can conveniently attend.

It is essential to determine the legal requirements that may influence collaborative structure and process. Although open and visible decisionmaking throughout the course of collaboration is desirable (Kenney *et al.* 2000, Wondolleck and Yaffee 2000), agency representatives must clearly examine and define sideboards on their role in the collaboration. Missions and laws among fire protection and land management agencies vary (Hummel and Freet 1999); accordingly, collaborators must work within the confines of policies separating agency roles and responsibilities (NWCG 1999). Formal agreements such as a Memorandum of Understanding or Agreement help avoid later, unanticipated problems by gaining approval for collaborative fire planning and clarifying potential legal issues (NWCG 1999).

Goals may be more clearly apparent in wildland fire and fuels management and constituency issues may not be as complex as in other natural resource issues, but process issues—ground rules, task groups, and roles for participating in public meetings, workshops, and outreach—still must be addressed. Meeting management and communication among group members between meetings were found to be critical in one fire planning process (Shaffer and Shipley 2002). Although some collaborations take years, establishing realistic timeframes is important for fire collaboration (NWCG 1999).

Learning: Sharing Information and Building Relationships

Information sharing is not only gathering data about the issue and developing a common knowledge base; it is also learning more about one another—exploring participants' interests and values, and building trust (USDI 2000). The current fire risk and prevention situation may have already been independently analyzed by each member of the collaboration, but the identification of hazardous fuels that could increase the spread and intensity of a wildland fire across ownership boundaries is best done collaboratively. An especially important opportunity is to define "values at risk" from wildfire. Citizens can contribute information about specific values and places they want protected, and work together to identify hazards and strategies for fuel reduction and community preparedness in their neighborhoods (Everett in press).

Implementation: Action to Achieve Goals

The ultimate goal of a collaborative partnership is to accomplish something on the ground. It is not difficult to agree upon the need to reduce wildland fire risk; however, it is more challenging to reach agreement about how and where to reduce fuels.

The Bureau of Land Management supported the Applegate Fire Plan by coordinating the use of its Slashbuster on projects on Federal, county, and private land.

Implementation may involve developing a set of management alternatives or creating a restoration or thinning project reflecting the group's common vision. This task requires agreement and support by the collaborating group, communities of interests, and those in authority. Conflicts may emerge. A focus on project outcomes helps to mitigate conflicting personalities or constituencies (Wondolleck and Yaffee 1994).

Photo credit: Bureau of Land Management

Outcome issues can be addressed by determining how the final decision or outcomes will be implemented (Blumberg 1999, Dukes and Firehock 2001) or by maintaining an "outside enforcement" of decisions (Britell 2003). Recordkeeping and other mechanisms for ensuring accountability are important for keeping players and the broader public informed of planned actions (USDI and Sonoran Institute 2000).

Funding needs to be secured, along with processes for coordinated implementation across administrative boundaries. It may be necessary at this juncture to formalize some relationships, creating a contract between stakeholders to ensure that plans are implemented (Bentrup 2001) and meeting requirements for receiving grants and other sources of funding.

Reflection: Monitoring and Evaluation

Monitoring and evaluation are two means of determining the effectiveness of both the collaborative process itself and collaboratively developed projects (Conley and Moote 2003, Dukes and Firehock 2001, Selin *et al.* 2000, Wondolleck and Yaffee 2000). These terms are often used interchangeably, but are in fact very different actions. Monitoring refers to the process of gathering data on a process or project and involves the repeated measurement of variables over time to determine if actions have caused changes or trends. Evaluation refers to the interpretation of these data and is used to judge the effectiveness of a process or program by comparing it to specific predetermined standards.

Monitoring is often found to be the most difficult area for groups to address adequately, because they may not recognize early enough the

Before entering into a collaborative process, it is important to consider the following (London 1995):

- Collaboration is time-consuming and not suitable for problems that require quick and decisive action.
- Power inequalities among the parties can derail the process.
- The norms of consensus and joint decisionmaking sometimes require that the common good take precedence over the interests of a few.
- Collaboration works best in small groups—the process can break down in groups that are large.
- Collaboration is meaningless without power to implement final decisions.

importance of gathering baseline data or identifying measurable objectives (Bentrup 2001). Monitoring is important for building accountability and support as well as for determining whether a project is working. Accountability is a key issue since wildfire and fuels management has become so politically charged. For example, the Applegate Fire Plan monitors perceptions of both participating agency representatives and local residents (Sturtevant and Corson 2003), as well as environmental impacts of projects. Because monitoring is so important to collaboration, a detailed discussion of how to monitor and evaluate collaborative partnerships is provided in appendix B.

Final Thoughts on Process

As mentioned above, collaborations go through these stages differently, and participants may find they are going through a labyrinth rather than an orderly process. Participants' expectations will need to be constantly monitored and managed to maintain involvement and support. Outcomes will reflect how challenges are resolved at each juncture. Because new issues arise and focus may change, the need for collaboration must initially be clearly and compellingly defined (Moote 2003). To succeed, it is important that all parties about to enter into collaboration understand the limitations of the process

(London 1995), and the literature is replete with conditions under which collaboration is not advised (Dukes and Firehock 2001, Kenney 2000, Moote 2003, USDA 2000, USDI 2000, Wondolleck and Yaffee 2000). However, by carefully considering the issues and context for collaboration, the barriers that may arise, and the essential elements of collaboration, wildland fire and fuel management staff can initiate powerful collaborations to accomplish their objectives.

The literature suggests many conditions under which collaboration will not work (Dukes and Firehook 2001, Kenney 2000, Moote 2003, USDA 2000, USDI 2000, Wondolleck and Yaffee 2000):

- History of extreme or unresolved conflict among key interests

- Lack of clear or realistic direction or goals

- Collaboration only for instrumental reasons, goals too specific

- Members not willing to make a commitment or compromise

- Key interests or decisionmakers not involved

- Partnership not needed because one entity can achieve goals alone

- Unequal partnership, some stand to benefit more than others

- Too short a deadline or need for immediate resolution

- Lack of resources (including institutional support)

- Financial and time commitments outweigh potential benefits

- Legal restrictions and too limited a decision space

- Constitutional issues or legal precedents sought

If these conditions do exist, it may be best to consider a process other than collaboration to proceed with the project.

Challenges to Building and Sustaining Collaboration

Getting the right people with a diverse array of interests and assets to the table, especially given potentially conflicting motives and goals, can be difficult. It is essential that all feel they have something to gain in order to invest, share, and compromise. Wildland fire has the advantage of being a common enemy; fuel reduction is a mutual goal around which players can communicate and establish trust: "after a while you realize both sides are in something they don't want to be in and can identify with each other" (Sturtevant and Corson 2003).

In this section we discuss challenges to collaboration in terms of three collaborative capacities, or capabilities, for collaborative action. These assets or contextual elements can be necessary for individuals, communities, and agencies to successfully collaborate. The first collaborative capacity we will discuss is individual participatory capacity—the willingness of people to become involved, communicate meaningfully, and follow through with actions necessary for successful collaboration. Second is community capacity—the collective resources and skills within a community that can drive and sustain a collaboration. And finally, we address institutional capacity—the authorities, culture, or characteristics of an organization that facilitate collaborative action.

We present this information with a focus on the Forest Service Ranger, Fire Management Officer, or other staff involved in building collaborative relationships to facilitate wildland fire and fuels management. However, anyone can use this information to build capacity in areas they feel are critical to the success of their project.

Challenges to Building and Sustaining Participatory Capacity

The "public" nature of Federal public forest lands poses a challenge to collaboration on wildland fire and fuels management. If people with local knowledge and perspectives, or others interested in the issues, are not included in the collaborative process, the process may be considered illegitimate, resulting in an inability to enact plans due to administrative appeals or legal action (Coggins 1999, McCloskey 1999, Singleton 2002). Nonparticipants have veto power in that they can enter the process late and reverse its movement. This can occur if they enter as participants who cannot support earlier collaborative visions or consensus agreements (Sturtevant and Lange 1995), if they file appeals or protests against collaborative projects, or solicit other political pressures to block a decision (Brick et al. 2001, Germain et al. 2001, Smith and McDonough 2001, Wondolleck and Yaffee 2000).

There are many reasons why agencies, groups, and individuals may resist collaboration. These reasons can be found in a common body of literature, often representing an environmental viewpoint (Blumberg 1999; Blumberg and Knuffke 1998; Brick et al. 2001; Britell 2003; Coggins 1999, 2001;

"Public participation is the process by which public concerns, needs, and values are incorporated into governmental decision making. Public participation is two-way communication, with the overall goal of better decisions, supported by the public."
(Creighton 1992, p. 12)

Diduck and Sinclair 2002; Duane 1997; Dukes and Firehock 2001; Germain *et al.* 2001; Ingles *et al.* 1999; Kenney 2000; Lowrie and Greenburg 2001; McCloskey 1996, 1999; Southern Utah Wilderness Alliance 1994; Williams and Ellefson 1996, 1997).

Reasons for Nonparticipation

A review of the literature mentioned above reveals two broad categories of reasons why individuals and groups do not participate. Individual stakeholders, such as landowners and community residents, as well as many interest groups, do not participate because they doubt the effectiveness of their participation. They may lack the resources to participate fully, or they may believe there is something in the collaborative process itself that will limit the effectiveness of their participation. People or groups may also refuse to participate because of a perceived discrepancy between their or their constituencies' values or ideology and the goals of the collaboration. Of course, some do not participate in a collaborative process simply because they were not invited or were unaware of the process (Rickenbach and Reed 2002, Walker and Daniels 2001).

> *The "public" nature of Federal public forest lands poses a challenge to collaboration on wildland fire and fuels management.*

We have organized the various reasons for noncollaboration into eight general categories. By understanding these concerns, collaborative groups can anticipate and work to overcome some of them.

Lack of resources: Research reports that potential participants share a concern about a lack of time, dollars, or skills to fully participate in a collaborative process. Federal land managers are concerned not only about the availability of these resources, but also whether they have the legal resources in terms of the laws and authorities to collaborate. Local and regional officials may also resist collaboration because they lack these necessary resources (Webler *et al.* 2003). Citizens' concerns extend to practical matters such as being able to afford to take time off from work or pay for a babysitter. They may also hesitate because they believe they lack the experience to participate or do not understand technical issues or the collaborative process (Daniels and Walker 2001).

Lack of technical expertise: Challenges of agency-layperson communication are particularly evident when communication centers on technical or scientific issues. Walker and Daniels (2001) contend that both citizens and scientists are interested in using the "best available science" when making natural resource management decisions. However, this may be a difficult task if managers, scientists, and citizens cannot agree on the meaning of restoration, nature, ecological integrity, or other environmentally related words and concepts.

According to researchers, most public managers deal with complex, cross-jurisdictional issues, and therefore must be able to operate in several different interorganizational networks to be effective. No manager can be expected to be conversant in all of the topics, but increasingly they are expected to be able to communicate across several disciplines, including law, finance, planning, engineering, and marketing (Arganoff and McGuire 1999, p. 21).

Concerns about process: The collaborative process itself may keep people from participating. Citizens, environmentalists, and Federal land managers may not participate because they see the collaborative process as exclusive or unfair in representation; the collaborative process may be seen as not representing public or scientific interests. They also may be uncomfortable with the meeting setting and methods of communication (Daniels and Walker 2001, Webler *et al.* 2003). Individuals involved in collaborative processes may tire from being repeatedly asked to participate in public involvement, collaboration, or other participatory activities and eventually drop out of all processes (Diduck and Sinclair 2002).

Literature states that potential participants may be reluctant to become involved in a collaborative process because they view the process itself as a "show," believing that the agency supporting the process has already made a decision and participation will not make an on-the-ground difference (Britell 2003, Southern Utah Wilderness Alliance 1994). Local officials have also been reported as expressing concern that involvement will not make a difference (Budd-Falen 1996, Webler *et al.* 2003). Some see industry interests as having co-opted the process (McCloskey 1996), and others question whether there is sufficient scientific backing (Blumberg 1999). They may also see the process as a way to delay new action or initiatives and maintain the status quo (Coggins 2001). Finally, public land managers, including those responsible for wildland fire and fuels management, may not be comfortable working in a collaborative setting.

"Today's managing occurs routinely at or outside of the boundaries of the home organization ... part of the routine is dealing with outside forces."
(Arganoff and McGuire 1999, p. 22)

Legal considerations for collaboration: Several different reasons for not participating in collaborative processes involve perceptions of the roles of laws and regulations. Reference has already been made to the lack of participation by Federal land managers because they feel that various laws or regulations actually limit or prevent their participation (Kenney *et al.* 2000, Rieke 1998).

Some people think that collaboration, if used to replace current decisionmaking processes, encourages agency representatives to disobey Federal laws and regulations, weakening Federal statutes and allowing public officials to abdicate some of their responsibilities (Coggins 2001, Kenney 2000). People with this perspective also question who will be held accountable for the final decision (Singleton 2002).

Some may prefer what are perceived as the checks and balances provided by the existing system, particularly in regards to public participation in decisionmaking. They may also believe that litigation and appeals based on NEPA mandates and other existing rules and regulations are more efficient and effective than collaborative processes (Britell 2003, Germain *et al.* 2001).

Landowners and private citizens offer yet another perspective on collaboration and existing laws and regulations. They have been reported as fearing that an outcome of collaboration will change the status quo with regard to property and water rights (Rickenbach 2002). They worry that collaboration might require divulging natural resource conditions on their private lands, which will result in new or additional regulations (Waage 2003, Williams and Ellefson 1996, 1997).

Appeals and veto power: The "public" nature of Federal public forestlands poses another challenge to collaboration on wildland fire and fuels management—a challenge that combines concerns discussed above about the process and laws. This is the ability of one person to halt the process. If people with local knowledge and perspectives, or others interested in the issues, are not included in the collaborative process, the process may be considered illegitimate, and these nonparticipants can then stop projects or other collaborative action through administrative appeals or legal action (Coggins 1999, McCloskey 1999). Nonparticipants can have veto power when they enter the process late and reverse its movement. This can occur if they (1) enter as participants who will not support earlier collaborative visions or consensus agreements (Sturtevant and Lange 1995), (2) file appeals or protests against collaborative projects, (3) solicit other political pressures to block a decision (Brick *et al.* 2001, Smith and McDonough 2001). Potential collaboration participants who have knowledge or experience with this exercise of power may refuse further involvement in collaborative activities for fear of a project-stalling or project-ending action.

Concerns about goals: Many contemplating involvement in a collaborative process may be concerned about whether the process will succeed in achieving individual, agency, or societal goals. Some individuals do not participate because they doubt that collaboration will enhance environmental protection (Coughlin *et al.* 1999, Rickenbach and Reed 2002). Local officials concerned about enhancing environmental protection may not participate because the goals of the collaborative do not include other vital community interests such as community stability (Lowrie and Greenburg 2001, Webler *et al.* 2003). Federal land managers concerned about environmental protection may question whether the collaborative will help them achieve high priority objectives of the agency (Blumberg and Knuffke 1998).

Concerns about trust: Some local officials report resistance to collaboration because citizens do not trust the agency that is perceived as controlling the process (Lowrie and Greenburg 2001, Webler *et al.* 2003). Local citizens may have similar concerns about trusting the process or players (Brick and Cawley 1996, Williams and Ellefson 1997). However, just as a lack of trust can encourage nonparticipation so can the presence of trust. Some report that local citizens and landowners trust the agency to work alone, or trust others to represent their interests in the collaborative process, so they feel no need to participate (Diduck and Sinclair 2002, Lange 2001).

Yet for many, a general philosophy of mistrust pervades, particularly for landowners and environmentalists and for some local and regional officials (Brick and Cawley 1996, Coughlin 1999, Lowrie and Greenburg 2001).

Concerns over constituency support: Local officials may not participate in collaborative processes because they believe that constituency support is lacking (Lange 2001, Lowrie and Greenburg 2001). Individuals may also hesitate to participate because, while they are there as representatives of a group, they lack authority or constituency support to do so. For example, an environmentalist may not feel able to commit to a course of action for the public or community interest, unlike a representative of a company or agency (Dukes and Firehock 2001). They also may believe that someone else is representing their stakeholder group or interests (Diduck and Sinclair 2002), even though their views may differ (Lange 2001).

One approach to ensuring effective stakeholder participation in collaborative groups is taking people to the field in order to ground their core values in site-specific fuel management options.

Enhancing Participation

Blahna and Yonts-Shepard (1989) reviewed the literature and various regulations and identified five criteria for effective stakeholder participation: involvement should be conducted early; it should be maintained throughout the planning process; input should be representative of all interested citizens; agencies should use personal forms of public involvement rather than "non-personal communications," such as mass public meetings; and they should maintain a transparent process. Early participation in the decision-making process increases satisfaction with the process and outcomes because these activities promote interactions

between the agency and stakeholders (Germain *et al.* 2001, Ingles *et al.* 1999, Wondolleck and Yaffee 2000). Explicit discussion of participants' individual and collective goals in collaboration can help address trust issues, including concerns about process, decisionmaking authority, and veto power (Moote and Becker 2004).

Participants attach diverse values and meanings to forest land, many of which are deeply held. These values and meaning will affect perceptions of wildland fire and fuels management projects. Participant involvement in a collaborative process is not simply a matter of generating "public acceptance" for fuels management or other projects, but is a complex negotiation and possible redefinition of core values. Fostering active, consistent member participation is an essential capacity for collaboration because it ensures that a broad diversity of voices, perspectives, values, and meanings have an opportunity to be expressed and considered during the decision process. The inability to foster active, consistent stakeholder participation can jeopardize even the most scientifically credible fuels management program.

Challenges for Building and Sustaining Community Capacity

"Deliberate attention to building community capacity ensures that a collaborative endures."
(Cestero 1999, p. 75)

We introduced the concept of community capacity earlier as one of the benefits of collaboration. Here we discuss how to build and sustain community capacity. Community capacity is the "combined influence of a community's commitment, resources and skills that can be deployed to build on community strengths and address community problems and opportunities" (Aspen Institute 1996, Introduction 1). The building blocks of community capacity can be defined as a set of assets possessed by individuals, organizations, and institutions within a community (Beaulieu 2002) or as a specific set of characteristics or attributes present within a community (Burns and Richard 2002). Community capacity is an important component to understand because, for wildfire and fuels management to be effective over the long term, a community must be able to sustain involvement in wildfire and fuels management activities into the future. Federal resources and expertise cannot be everywhere all the time; communities need to recognize and embrace their shared responsibility for wildfire and fuels management.

"Community capacity is the interaction of human capital, organizational resources, and social capital existing within a given community that can be leveraged to solve collective problems and improve or maintain the well-being of a given community. It may operate through informal social processes and/or organized effort."
(Chaskin 2001)

Successful collaborations build on community capacity. But what if a community appears to have little capacity? Some look at this question from the perspective that no matter how impoverished, divided, or broken down a community is, some amount of capacity exists, with the potential for building more (Aspen Institute 1996, Beaulieu 2002). Building community capacity is a matter of identifying and fostering community strengths, and of working with and strengthening areas of weakness.

Building Community Capacity

Activities that create and sustain a web of relationships that cross political, economic, and other boundaries will promote community capacity. These activities might include participation in civic organizations, volunteer work, Chamber of Commerce activities, or church socials. Strengthening social capital might also be conceived as strengthening the settings where informal daily life takes place, such as libraries, cafes, or community centers (Oldenburg as cited in London 1995), where trust and relationships can be built, thereby creating a "civic infrastructure that lends itself to collaboration."

> *Community capacity is an important component to understand because, for wildfire and fuels management to be effective over the long term, a community must be able to sustain involvement in wildfire and fuels management activities into the future.*

Community capacity building can also take place through more formal means. Here, it is important to remember that building community capacity is about increasing the skills and resources not only of individuals, but also of agencies, organizations, and networks within the community, as well as those outside that affect the community.

Chaskin (2001) categorize community-building approaches into four different types. One is leadership development. Fostering collaborative leadership skills is an important form of capacity building that is mentioned by most sources (Chaskin 2001, University of Kansas 2003). Such workshops may promote skills and competencies such as multiculturalism or inclusion.

Other categories of capacity-building activities suggested by Chaskin (2001) include "organizational development, community organizing and fostering collaborative relations between organizations" (p. 299). Organizational capacity building focuses on the institutions within the community—creating new ones, strengthening existing ones, and finding ways to support them. Community organizing historically has meant coalition building and working from a grassroots approach. And fostering collaborative relations means communicating effectively, sharing a vision, and working together.

Schindler-Rainman and Lippit (1993, p. 41) offer a set of eight recommendations for building community capacity by developing effective collaborative groups:

- Involve community leaders from a wide range of "functional sectors." (Public safety, recreation, social welfare, education, health, economic, political, religious, mass media, arts/culture.)

- Find ways to recruit, motivate, and mobilize the young, middle-aged, and elderly; women and men; established and and informal leadership; advantaged and disadvantaged populations; racial, national, and ethnic minorities; handicapped community groups.

- Develop new ways for the polarized, distrustful segments of the community to be included...and therefore to communicate more openly and frequently and learn new designs and skills for collaboration.

- Develop methods and situations that demonstrate the value of differences of traditions, ideas, beliefs, needs, and expectations as a resource.

- Help people learn the skills required to develop collaborative networks and support their effective functioning, including development and training of internal "change agents."

- Increase the awareness, sensitivity, and skills of professionals and members to enable them to engage underutilized citizen volunteers and groups.

- Develop procedures for linking ad hoc initiators and groups into the ongoing structures, operating traditions and "continuities" of the community.

- Develop commitment, designs, and mechanisms for followup work on goals, intentions, and plans discussed in the initial [stages of the collaboration] (p. 41).

Indicators of community capacity

How do you know when you've succeeded in building community capacity? "Measuring Community Capacity Building: A Workbook in Progress for Rural Communities" (Aspen Institute 1996) lists eight outcomes that indicate community capacity building is taking place:

- Expanding, diverse, inclusive citizen participation
- Expanding leadership base
- Strengthened individual skills
- Widely shared understanding and vision
- Strategic community agenda
- Consistent, tangible progress toward goals
- More effective community organizations
- Better resource use by the community

It is important to remember that community capacity building, just like collaboration, is a process. No two communities, or the individuals and organizations that make up the community, have the same amount of capacity.
Although capacity building can sometimes progress rapidly, at other times it
can be painstakingly slow and tedious (Beaulieu 2002), and it requires commitment, initiative, direction, and determination (Aspen Institute 1996).

Challenges for Institutional Capacity

Various factors influence whether an agency or organization is able or willing to
take part in the participatory process. There is no shortage of literature faulting
the Forest Service for failing to support collaboration. The Forest Service is aware
of the challenges to collaboration that managers face and has taken steps to address them. In appendix C
the reader will find the recommendations of Chief Bosworth's Partnership Authorities Workgroup. Below
we discuss eight factors often perceived as limiting the Forest Service's capacity for collaboration (and that
of some other agencies and organizations).

*Local citizens lead activities
related to the Applegate Fire
Plan, creating a diverse and
expanded leadership base in
the community.*

Laws and Authorities

The complex array of laws and policies governing Forest Service actions has created confusing, and in
some cases, conflicting guidance on when, where, and how it is appropriate for the agency to collaborate with others. Some managers are understandably reluctant to collaborate for fear of legal repercus-
sions. In addition, some Federal laws deter private entities from collaboration. However, there is one
law almost universally cited as a barrier to collaboration—the Federal Advisory Committee Act of 1972
(FACA), which is discussed more fully in appendix D. Some policy analysts say that "FACA Fear" and
confusion over the role and responsibilities of Federal land managers have caused managers to be
unusually conservative in their collaborative efforts (Loucks and Kostishack 2001, Wondolleck and
Yaffee 2000). The Healthy Forests Restoration Act of 2003 (PL 108-148) explicitly addresses this issue
by stating that, "the Federal Advisory Committee Act… shall not apply to the planning process and
recommendation concerning community wildfire protection plans." (Section 103.b.2)

*"Inconsistent interpretation of
authorities between regions
gives partners and agency
employees … the impression
that certain partnerships are
only possible in some places."
(Loucks and Kostishack 2001, p. 8)*

Fear of invoking the National Environmental Policy Act of 1969 (NEPA) and Endangered Species
Act of 1973 (ESA) discourages some private landowners from partnering with Federal agencies on
cross-jurisdictional projects (Loucks and Kostishack 2001), and the Sherman Antitrust Act has been
interpreted by some to mean that private companies cannot collaborate in collective landscape
planning, and that contracting officers should not work too closely with contractors in stewardship
contracting (Wondolleck and Yaffee 2000). Similarly, the Freedom of Information Act may discourage

private parties from sharing sensitive information with Federal agencies (Loucks and Kostishack 2001). The Healthy Forests Restoration Act explicitly addresses some of these concerns by exempting the development of community wildfire protection plans from both FACA and NEPA. In addition, the growing number of effective collaborations among public and private landowners and others suggests that, as with FACA, the laws themselves are less a barrier to collaboration than is fear of Federal regulation in general.

Procedural Delays (Bureaucracy)

The second challenge to building institutional capacity for collaboration is procedural delays. For example, FACA, NEPA, ESA, and the National Forest Management Act of 1976 (NFMA) are said to limit the agency's ability to collaborate with the private sector and local government because their complex procedures require large investments of time and money in project planning. "The environmental laws [of the 1960s and 1970s] spawned thousands of pages of regulations and administrative rules… These requirements included a stream of predecisional consultations and analyses, often followed by postdecisional appeals and litigation" (USDA 2002, p. 12).

Many policy scholars and collaborators say the laws themselves are not the problem—the problem lies in the delays inherent in their implementation, which are sometimes due to agency regulations but which also stem from excessive environmental analyses by agency personnel anxious to cover themselves in the case of potential appeals and litigation (Loucks and Kostishack 2001, USDA 2002). By the 1990s, Forest Service line officers were "caught in a procedural quagmire" of project planning and review (USDA 2002, p. 12).

Forest Service appeals, which allow citizens to challenge a line officer's decision to proceed with a project, are said to cause further unnecessary delays. In addition, the ability of any interest to file an appeal after a decision has been made discourages some groups from collaborating (USDA 2002).

There is some hope for cutting the bureaucratic red tape that can delay fuels management projects in the passage of new regulations under the Healthy Forests Initiative and implementation of the Health Forests Restoration Act of 2003. The Act and new regulations provide administrative improvements that are meant to ensure more timely decisions, greater efficiency, and better projects (U.S. Government nd). Finally, as noted above, open discussion of potential bureaucratic delays early in the collaborative process may help collaborators plan on realistic timelines and mitigate frustration down the line when delays actually occur.

"Frequently, these memorandums, agreements, cost-shares, and contracts involve excessive paperwork, follow-up reports, and legal language and are often too difficult to understand. Many times the agreements themselves take too long to complete, complicate a simple project, cost too much in salaries to write, and in effect scare off our collaborators and partners. … Involving the public in our programs and management is often hampered by excessive detail and red tape."

(Forest Supervisor quoted in Wondolleck and Yaffee 2000, p. 54)

Funding Issues

Although collaborative resource management is said to reduce management costs by allowing organizations to pool resources and develop joint management strategies, substantial costs are also associated with collaborative group processes, most notably extremely large time demands placed on managers and other collaborators (Arganoff and McGuire 1999, Wondolleck and Yaffee 2000). These funding issues can become barriers to maintaining institutional capacity for collaboration.

Research on collaborative groups has found that stable, long-term, and flexible funding is closely correlated with a group's effectiveness (Born and Genskow 2000, Wondolleck and Yaffee 2000, Yaffee *et al.* 1996). The Forest Service is chronically short of funding for collaborative efforts, and what funding is available is inconsistent (e.g., long turnaround times for grant approval, findings not distributed in a timely manner, funding limited to one year because of agency budget) (Loucks and Kostishack 2001, Sustainable Northwest *et al.* 2002).

Forest Service budgets are driven by line items, and there are no line items for collaborative efforts—or even for fundamental agency activities like public involvement and collaborative stewardship (Loucks and Kostishack 2001). Managers have little flexibility to redirect appropriations, leaving many collaborative partnerships or projects unfunded because they do not fit within the agency's budgeting structure (Wondolleck and Yaffee 2000). Another problem is that much of the funding available for collaborative efforts is available only in large amounts; funding needs to be scaled to the needs of rural communities and institutionalized into standing programs (Sustainable Northwest *et al.* 2002).

Agency fiscal procedures can also limit collaboration. Many community groups and small nonprofit organizations report difficulty meeting the funding match required for Forest Service cost-share agreements (Baker and Kusel 2003, Loucks and Kostishack 2001). Although the law authorizing collaborative cost-share grants does not specify what percentage of the match must be provided by cooperators, the Forest Service manual instructs agency personnel to negotiate a dollar-for-dollar match (Baker and Kusel 2003). Furthermore, Forest Service rules generally do not allow managers to contribute funds to a project before its implementation. Instead, the agency generally reimburses for work after it is completed (Loucks and Kostishack 2001). But agency partners, especially small rural governments and organizations, are not likely to be able to carry large project costs.

Agency History and Culture

For most of the 20th century, the Forest Service operated in a government that believed in the separation of administration and politics, and left management decisions to agencies, which were staffed by highly

> "It is simply unrealistic to expect an effective network ... to be sustained without substantial investment by the government to provide for program management, group coordination, and cost-sharing for on-the-ground work."
>
> *(Curtis* et al. *2002, p. 1207)*

trained specialists. Agency accountability was achieved through written rules, standard operating procedures, and professional standards, and enforced through a hierarchical system in which decisions and commands came from a centralized authority in Washington, DC. The Washington Office was accountable to Congress and the Administration, but for the most part, the agency had autonomous decision-making authority within its jurisdiction (USDA 2002, Weber 2003, Wondolleck and Yaffee 2000).

"A lot of this goes against my training."
(Forest Service silviculturalist quoted in Wondolleck and Yaffee 2000, p. 62)

In the 1960s and 1970s, as public hearings and comment periods became commonplace and the courts liberalized their rules governing citizen lawsuits, the concept of agency accountability expanded to include individuals and interest groups that could demonstrate standing in the courts (Weber 1999). Public comment periods, appeals, and litigation did not encourage collaboration, however; instead, they led the agency to focus on rigorous recordkeeping to defend its decisions in the face of thousands of appeals and lawsuits (USDA 2002, Wondolleck and Yaffee 2000).

Forest managers' training and organizational history have taught them to be self-reliant and even suspicious of outsider input, leaving many reluctant to collaborate with citizens, interest groups, or even other government agencies as partners (Loucks and Kostishack 2001). Yet recent trends in American governance emphasize increased public participation, and the public now expects the agency to engage in "nonhierarchical, place-based networks in which government, citizens, and organized stakeholders cooperate and negotiate" land management issues (Weber 1999, p. 456). Collaborators have come to expect that agency managers will be "accountable" to their group; and to many, accountability has come to mean "the ability of government to actually deliver on promises" (Weber 1999, p. 459).

The differences between agency and public expectations of collaboration can be profound and can lead to unfair or inappropriate accusations of uncollaborative behavior. A public perception that collaboration means jointly developing creative management plans conflicts with an agency perception that collaboration should be project-specific and not extend to making management decisions (Moote and Becker 2003). The result of such a scenario may be accusations that Forest Service personnel are indifferent or hostile to collaboration, as when interest groups and individuals report participating in scoping meetings, hearings, and public comment periods only to see the agency make management decisions that they believe went against the expressed interests of the public and the perceived best interest of the environment (Wondolleck and Yaffee 2000).

As mentioned earlier, although inconsistent expectations of collaboration can present significant challenges, they can also be overcome by frank and open discussions of what collaboration means to all parties in the current context.

Internal Communication

Lack of communication within an agency or organization can further impede collaboration. For example, in the Forest Service, National Forest System staff generally are unaware of existing networks of collaboration between State and Private Forestry's Cooperative Forestry staff and local communities—even when staff from both units are located in the same office (Baker and Kusel 2003, Frentz *et al.* 1999). Timber contracting officers and service contracting officers rarely work together, yet new contracting authorities require an understanding of both sets of procedures (Sustainable Northwest *et al.* 2002)

Line officers' confusion over authorities has also been attributed to breakdown in communication along the chain of command from the national to the forest and district level. Policy analysts cite cases of field staff claiming they do not have the authority to do something, while the Washington Office simultaneously claims they do (KenCairn 2000, Loucks and Kostishack 2001). The result is agency staff afraid to use existing authorities for fear they do not apply (Loucks and Kostishack 2001, Sustainable Northwest *et al.* 2002).

Aside from the delays and confusion, poor internal communication also increases the risk that higher levels in the agency will override or impede a collaborative decision negotiated at the local level, an action that has seriously undermined some collaborative efforts (KenCairn 2000). Individual forests have also been known to make decisions or set priorities that are inconsistent with cooperative agreements that have been set at the regional level (Loucks and Kostishack 2001).

Poor internal communication is exacerbated by the agency's practice of transferring line officers every few years, because institutional knowledge tends to leave an office with the individual. When key agency staff who have been participants in collaborative arrangements are transferred, collaborative groups find they must inform new personnel of existing agreements, or even renegotiate them. Enthusiasm for a collaborative effort may leave the office along with the individual who championed it within the agency (KenCairn 2000). One study that tracked 35 collaborative processes over a 3- to 5-year period found that personnel changes affected 42 percent of the original cases (Wondolleck and Yaffee 2000). In a few forestry collaboratives, replacement or transfer of key agency personnel caused the entire effort to fail (Loucks and Kostishack 2001).

To some extent, improving internal communication is an individual responsibility of all agency staff, but the Forest Service has attempted to provide guidance and mentoring through groups like the Partnership Task Force, which was chartered in June 2002 "to assist practitioners and partners by

"It only takes one bulldozer operator unclear about where a road is supposed to go or not go, one chainsaw operator unclear about the diameter limit mark, one marking crew confused about a spotted owl nest location to make a high-profile mistake, destroying the credibility of a negotiated, consensus-developed collaborative project [that took] months or years to develop. Similarly, it only takes one person in a District office [who is confused or concerned about] a collaborative project to stall or spread disinformation that significantly delays or damages the credibility of such projects."
(KenCairn 2000, p. 10)

fostering an organizational culture that cultivates and expands partnership capacity and by streamlining the internal work process of the agency" (Loucks 2002, p. 27).

Interorganizational Cooperation

Historically, Federal agencies have not reached out to local governments to help them implement projects, but local government participation in environmental management is increasingly being recognized as critical to good outcomes.

"Centralized and unresponsive agencies, like the Forest Service, tend to be unreliable partners."

(Thomas 1999, p. 544)

A study of interagency coordination for wildland fire management found that only the firefighting aspects were well coordinated and recommended that the agencies create more inclusive and more effective interagency work groups (Fairbanks *et al.* 2001). Another study suggests that Federal managers should make an effort to engage local governments for three reasons (Webler *et al.* 2003). First, local officials are instrumental to ensuring regulations are implemented at the local level. Second, local officials have unique insights into local needs, concerns, and resources that can be valuable to Federal managers. Finally, local officials can have a major influence on community support or opposition to State and Federal policies.

Research on collaborative resource management groups has found that the more successful are those to which agencies have dedicated staff time (Imperial and Hennessey 2000). Unfortunately, staff time and decisionmaking authority are in short supply in Forest Service field offices (Wondolleck and Yaffee 2000). In addition, Forest Service employees who attempt to collaborate and implement innovative ideas may not be rewarded or recognized for their efforts. The agency's employee performance evaluation criteria seldom include collaboration or partnership activities; line officers who want to get ahead in the agency have little incentive to risk spending their time on new collaborative endeavors (Loucks and Kostishack 2001, Wondolleck and Yaffee 2000). In some cases, risk takers have been actively censured for engaging in collaborative activities (KenCairn 2000).

According to public administration experts, "the most important change in administrative functions over the last century, in both the public and private sectors, is the dramatic rise in organizational interdependence" (Arganoff and McGuire 1999, p.19). To help managers adapt to this new work environment, "leading corporations and government agencies" create a "learning environment" based on "sharing best practices, rewarding successful action and initiative, and working cooperatively to solve problems. They avoid punitive "scapegoating" and instead focus on enhancing performance and employee morale" (Fairbanks *et al.* 2001, p. xxvi).

Lack of Trust and Accountability

Policy scholars say that, for a process to be trusted, it must be legitimate, credible, and fair. By legitimate they mean that a collaborative process and its activities satisfy legal mandates, are sanctioned by administrative procedure, have the support and commitment of the agency, and recognize other rights and authorities. By credible they mean that the collaborative process and its activities are grounded in the best available science and experiential knowledge. By fair they mean that the collaborative process and its activities are inclusive and representative, that everyone has equal access to information, and that decisionmaking criteria are mutually agreed on (Committee of Scientists 1999, Wondolleck and Yaffee 2000).

Managers' reluctance to collaborate, inconsistent messages to the partners about authorities, and reversed agency decisions exacerbate a climate of mistrust and escalate the public's demands for greater agency accountability to those with whom it collaborates. These issues are not unique to government agencies; increasingly, sociologists and political scientists studying collaborations are identifying a lack of accountability—of mechanisms for enforcing group standards and agreements—to be a major problem (Cigler 1999, Mandell 1999b, Weber 1999). Because of these issues of trust, as well as the reality that unscrupulous individuals can misuse collaborative processes, researchers suggest that collaborative efforts should focus "not just on building trust but rather on establishing predictability and reducing vulnerability" (Mandell 1999b, p. 13).

Research on watershed collaboratives has shown that the more successful groups are those that have developed mechanisms for monitoring activities and enforcing group decisions, whether through formal agreements or peer pressure (Born and Genskow 2000, Imperial and Hennessey 2001, Margerum 2001). In a study of interagency collaboration, Takahashi and Smutny (2001) found that an "emphasis on informality within and between agencies … contributed to conflict and miscommunication… [and] led to a lack of sanctioning when particular organizations engaged in behaviors that were deemed unacceptable by the other agencies," such as failure to show up at meetings or provide agreed-upon services (p. 147).

The policy analysis literature specific to forestry collaboratives resounds with calls for monitoring and evaluation of collaborative group processes and outcomes as a form of accountability among different parties (KenCairn 2000, Loucks and Kostishack 2001, Sustainable Northwest *et al.* 2002, Wondolleck and Yaffee 2000). In addition to providing a measure of accountability, monitoring and evaluation offer a mechanism by which the agency can document and learn from prior experiences in collaboration, reducing the risk that mistakes will be repeated.

"Across the United States, researchers consistently have found high levels of public distrust of federal forest and rangeland managers, which has led citizens to become leery of participation in agency ecosystem-based management programs."
(Schindler et al. *2002, p. 17)*

Policy Resources for Collaboration

Forest Service wildland fire and fuels management staff can draw on several policies to facilitate and support collaboration. These policy resources come and go with different initiatives and programs, so agency staff need to monitor what resources are currently available.

State and Private Forestry's Collaborative Forestry staff of the Forest Service has long collaborated with communities through its Economic Action Programs, Urban and Community Forestry Program, and Landowner Assistance Programs. Their ability to collaborate with local communities has expanded with an influx of funds from President Clinton's National Fire Plan that started in 2000. National forest line officers and staff too have access to a number of relatively new tools for collaboration, including new authorities under the Healthy Forests Restoration Act, the Wyden Amendment, the County Payments Act, stewardship contracting, and other new programs. In addition, the agency has many mechanisms by which it can partner with tribal, State, and local governments, private businesses, non-profit organizations, and individuals. Many of the new authorities, as well as innovative new uses for existing authorities, were developed in collaborative processes.

Healthy Forest Restoration Act

The Healthy Forest Restoration Act of 2003 (HFRA) specifically authorizes the Forest Service and the Bureau of Land Management to plan and conduct hazardous fuels reduction projects on Federal lands located in the wildland-urban interface or intermix community, or on lands where wildfire would threaten values in the interface or intermix community.

Initiatives such as HFRA encourage Federal agencies to conduct fuels reduction projects in the wildland-urban interface.

Several of the HFRA provisions specifically speak to the value and importance of collaboration, especially at the local community level. Section 104(d) states, "In order to encourage meaningful public participation in the identification and development of authorized hazardous fuels reduction projects, the Secretary concerned shall facilitate collaboration among governments and interested persons during the formulation of each authorized fuels reduction project in a manner consistent with the Implementation Plan." Under Title III of HFRA (Watershed Forestry Assistance), Section 302 instructs the Secretary of Agriculture to establish a watershed forestry cost-share program to help fund critical forest stewardship, watershed protection, and restoration needs. Such projects can specifically be developed through community-based planning, involvement, and action through State, local, and nonprofit organizations. Perhaps most significantly, the act places priority on restoration and fuels reduction

projects in areas identified by communities themselves in community wildfire protection plans (CWPP). Treatment areas identified in a collaboratively developed CWPP will receive priority funding over projects identified by the Federal agencies alone. Finally, HFRA provides for "a multiparty monitoring, evaluation, and accountability process" of Forest Service and BLM projects developed under the act. HFRA sets a new benchmark for collaboration in wildfire and fuels management.

HFRA also addresses concerns about bureaucratic delays by authorizing expedited environmental assessment, administrative appeals, and legal review fro hazardous fuels reduction projects on Federal land.

> *HFRA provides for "a multiparty monitoring, evaluation, and accountability process" of Forest Service and BLM projects developed under the act.*

National Fire Plan Authorities

The National Fire Plan (actually a series of government reports and agency strategies) was developed in part to address a lack of coordination among Federal, State, and local agencies responsible for fire management and suppression. "A key tenet of the National Fire Plan is coordination between government agencies at the federal, state, and local levels to develop strategies and carry out programs" (Kostishack and Rana 2002, p. 7). To emphasize this goal, Congress directed the Secretary of Agriculture to work with the Western Governors' Association to implement the 10-Year Comprehensive Strategy—A Collaborative Approach for Reducing Wildland Fire Risks to Communities and the Environment. Several of the objectives articulated in the 10-Year Strategy specifically call for agency collaboration with communities, including:

- Reduce wildland fire risk to communities and the environment for the long term.
- Promote a collaborative, community-based approach to wildland fire management that recognizes the importance of making key decisions at the local level.
- Promote community assistance.
- Hold collaboration, priority setting, and accountability as core guiding principles. (Kostishack and Rana 2002).

Since 2001, annual appropriations funding the National Fire Plan have given Forest Service managers authority to enter into procurement contracts, grants, and cooperative agreements with local nonprofits, Youth Conservation Corps, or small disadvantaged businesses to carry out hazardous fuels reduction activities on Federal lands and provide training and monitoring associated with those activities (Kostishack and Rana 2002). The National Fire Plan also increased funding to the State and Private Forestry programs.

Wyden Amendment

Legislation passed in 1998, commonly referred to as the Wyden Amendment (PL105-277), authorizes Forest Supervisors to enter into collaborative arrangements with other governmental or private entities, including landowners, to accomplish restoration, protection, and enhancement work on public or private lands, as long as that work is of high priority for the agency (USDA 2003b). The Wyden Amendment also allows the agency to spend appropriated dollars outside of the National Forest System boundaries (Loucks and Kostishack 2001, Sustainable Northwest *et al.* 2002, USDA and BLM 2001). This authority is delegated to Forest Supervisors and may be redelegated to District Rangers, but not to any other position. All appropriated funds are available for use under the Wyden Amendment, unless there is specific language in the appropriation that prohibits or restricts its use (USDA 2003b).

County Payments Bill

The purposes of the Secure Rural Schools and Community Self Determination Act of 2000, also known as the County Payments Bill, are:

1. to stabilize payments in lieu of taxes to counties to help pay for roads and schools,
2. to provide funding for projects that enhance forest ecosystem health and provide employment opportunities, and
3. to improve cooperative relationships among Federal land management agencies and those who use and care about the lands the agencies manage.

Counties that choose to receive their share of payments to States under a new formula established by this law are required to use 80 to 85 percent of the funds received on local schools and the county road program. The remaining 15 to 20 percent must be allocated to projects authorized under Title II or Title III of the new law. Title II projects either take place on Federal lands or benefit Federal lands. Title III projects are county projects that may include search and rescue, community service work camps, easement purchases, forest-related education opportunities, fire prevention and county planning, or cost-share for urban community forestry projects.

The County Payments Bill also requires the establishment of Resource Advisory Councils (RACs), advisory councils chartered under FACA that recommend projects to the Secretary of Agriculture for Title II funding and that also may advise counties on Title III projects.

Stewardship Contracting

Stewardship contracting, an authority that first became available through an appropriations bill rider in 1999, was designed to:

- encourage broad-based community collaboration,
- give contractors more flexibility,
- facilitate comprehensive ecosystem management,
- and help build a new workforce focused on forest health restoration and maintenance activities (Sustainable Northwest *et al.* 2002).

Collaboration is a requirement of every stewardship contract. In addition, the pilot program, which contracted 84 projects between 1999 and 2002, required multiparty monitoring of all stewardship contracting projects. Legislation passed in early 2003 extended stewardship contracting authorities—which include best-value contracting, designation by description/prescription (also known as end-results or performance-based contracting), multiyear contracts, exchange of goods for services, and receipt retention—to all lands managed by the Forest Service and Bureau of Land Management. The new legislation reinforces the directives to collaborate with local and State governments, nonprofit organizations, and other interested parties; allow contracts with youth groups and small businesses or microbusinesses; and consider benefits to local communities when awarding contracts. It also removes the requirement for project-level multiparty monitoring.

Economic Action Programs

Economic Action Programs, particularly the Rural Community Assistance Program, fund community capacity building for collaboration (Loucks 2002, Sustainable Northwest *et al.* 2002). "From the perspective of community forestry practitioners and supporters, [these programs are] some of the most effective tools communities and the Forest Service have for working together on efforts to build community capacity, support economic diversification, and foster the development of a forest stewardship-based economy" (Baker and Kusel 2003). The State and Private Forestry Branch of the Forest Service administers both the Economic Action and Rural Community Assistance programs.

> *The State and Private Forestry Branch of the Forest Service administers both the Economic Action and Rural Community Assistance programs.*

Forest Land Enhancement Program

Created in the 2002 Farm Bill (Farm Security and Rural Investment Act of 2002), the Forest Land Enhancement Program (FLEP) is intended "to establish a coordinated and cooperative Federal, State, and local sustainable forestry program for the establishment, management, maintenance, enhancement, and restoration of forests on nonindustrial private forest land" (Act). FLEP is a cost-share program that encourages the long-term sustainability of nonindustrial private forest lands. This program is implemented through State Foresters in coordination with State forest stewardship coordinating committees and in consultation with other stakeholders. Congress authorized

> *FLEP is a cost-share program that encourages the long-term sustainability of nonindustrial private forest lands.*

mandatory appropriations of $100 million for 5 years, to guarantee that cost-share assistance would be available to landowners (Rana 2002).

Fire Assistance Programs

In addition, appropriations for implementing the National Fire Plan have increased funding for specific programs that allow State and Private Forestry to partner with or fund State and local fire management efforts. These include:

- State Fire Assistance (authorizes the USDA Forest Service to cooperate with State Foresters to build State and local firefighting capacity, support fire hazard mitigation projects in the wildland-urban interface, and support Firewise workshops for homeowners)
- Volunteer Fire Assistance (authorizes the USDA Forest Service to cooperate with State Foresters to fund volunteer fire departments for training, improved communication, and equipment and protective clothing purchase).

A new assistance program, the Community and Private Land Fire Assistance Program, was developed under the National Fire Plan to promote firefighting efficiency at all levels on Federal and non-Federal lands and to protect communities from wildland fire threats. It also supports multiresource, landscape-level fire protection on Federal and non-Federal lands. This program is administered by the Forest Service and implemented through State Foresters in cooperation with Federal, State, and local agencies (Rana 2002).

Agency Mentors and Models

Managers often overlook the knowledge of people sitting at the next desk or working for the agency down the road who have been successful in developing collaborative partnerships. These individuals can be valuable sources of "lessons learned" on collaboration. Some agency personnel and former employees have developed collaborative stewardship training seminars and workshops (Baker and Kusel 2003). The Contracting Desk Guide is an example of a resource developed by agency contracting staff to help other contracting officers understand the expanding array of contracting authorities available to them (USDA 2002). The agency's recent practice of designating liaisons to multiagency projects and collaboratives and loaning Federal employees to its collaborators (Loucks and Kostishack 2001) is creating another pool of agency employees with networking experience.

The National Fire Plan Implementation Team, which works to coordinate fire management efforts within the agency, and the National Interagency Fire Center, which coordinates the fire and aviation resources of all relevant Federal agencies and fosters cooperative agreements with State, local, and tribal entities, are good examples of internal and external coordination and collaboration and resources that managers can turn to for assistance (Kostishack and Rana 2002).

Pilot projects and programs that have been testing new collaborative approaches—like the Four Corners Sustainable Forests Partnership in New Mexico, Arizona, Colorado, and Utah; the Blue Mountains Demonstration Area in Oregon; and the Collaborative Forest Restoration Program in New Mexico—are additional sources of managers with collaboration experience and examples of collaboration techniques. Experiments with stewardship contracting in the Blue Mountains Demonstration Area, for example, resulted in the development of Integrated Resource Contracts, now an agency model for stewardship contracting.

Keys to Successful Collaboration

Collaboration is not a panacea or a silver bullet (Pipkin and Doerksen 2000); it is not always effective or appropriate. From the earlier discussion of barriers to building participatory capacity, the charge to initiate collaborative associations to support wildland fire and fuels management may appear to be a "Mission Impossible." However, lessons can be learned from successful collaborations that can help overcome these barriers. Some issues can be anticipated and a plan can be developed for addressing them as they emerge.

Step-by-step guides to successful collaboration cannot suit the specific needs of every situation (Borrini-Feyerabend 1996), but many lessons are available from others' experiences. Some are essential for successful collaborations, others make the process easier, and others have resulted in better ecosystem projects. These essentials come from a number of sources:

- Prescriptions in how-to guides and training manuals for collaboration in the natural resource arena (BLM and Sonoran Institute 2000, Pipkin and Doerksen 2000, Sirmon 2001, USDA 1995, USDI 2000).
- Articles and case studies by collaboration process participants and facilitators (Daniels *et al.* 1996, Round Tables 1998, Shafer and Shipley 2002, USDA 2000).
- Comprehensive assessments by academics and researchers who have analyzed case studies (Leach and Pelkey 2001, Pipkin and Doerksen 2000, Wondolleck and Yaffee 2000); reviewed collaborative literature more generally (Mattessich *et al.* 2000); and questioned participants through mail surveys (Leach 2002, Paulson and Chamberlin 1998, Schuett *et al.* 2001, Williams and Ellefson 1996), interviews (Belden *et al.* 2001, Brunner *et al.* 2002, Carr *et al.* 1998) or during workshops (Loucks 2002, Propst and Rosan 1997).

The 11 essentials discussed below address many of the barriers to collaborative capacity and emphasize some of the tasks discussed earlier.

Focus on Community Context

To support collaborative fuels management across ownership boundaries, people need to understand that community context matters. The history of collaboration or cooperation in the community shapes current efforts (Mendez *et al.* 2003). Contentious, unresolved past conflict will hinder success (Moote 2003); collective past achievements will better position a community to address a common threat such as wildland fire (Sturtevant and Corson 2003).

Focus on Resource Stewardship

It is essential to build on the broader issue of resource stewardship. "Collaborative stewardship is most effective when practiced close to the ground" (USDA 2000, p. 13) and builds on community members'

Successful wildfire management collaborations build on the broader issue of resource stewardship.

attachment to place. Collaboratives stay on track and produce results on the land by keeping focus on a common landscape vision (TNC 2003) and by working toward a set of solutions with measurable outcomes. "Unless you can work toward the same goal, the process is unlikely to produce results. This does not mean, however, that each party needs to be motivated by the same reasons to work toward the goal" (Belden *et al.* 2001).

Focusing on resource stewardship creates a strong common bond among participants (Williams and Ellefson 1997), evoking emotions that can motivate landowners and other interested parties to join and take an active part in a partnership. The key is to connect these emotions to facts and data that participants can agree upon (Pipkin and Doerksen 2000), rather than rhetoric that can bog down the collaboration. Field trips help people connect to the land as well as to each other and move them past ideology to common attachment to place.

Focus on Appropriate Scale

It is essential to work at a scale appropriate to the community, a scale that evokes shared values, collective action, and sense of place—often neighborhoods or subwatersheds within a larger watershed.

Local, small projects work better than larger ones, but need to be broad enough to cover the ecosystem (Pipkin and Doerksen 2000). Fire managers may relate to watershed boundaries, but public interest and identity might work better at the neighborhood level (Sturtevant and Jakes 2003).

Curtis *et al.* (2002) noted that watershed groups function better at the local (community) scale than at the larger landscape (bioregional) scale, but others (Kenney 2000) suggested that intermediary or "umbrella" groups that work within a larger geographic area (rather than a watershed or community scale) can be important for integrating local groups and national groups and policymakers. "Umbrella groups may provide funding opportunities, administrative infrastructure, and general networking opportunities [that local groups] would otherwise not be able to realize" (Kenney 2000).

When talking about scale both geographic scale and temporal scale are important. Concerning the temporal scale, Leach *et al.* (2002) found that it typically "takes 48 months to achieve major milestones such as formal agreements and implementation of restoration, education, or monitoring projects." This correlates well with the observation that collaborative fisheries groups took 3 to 5 years to reach a level of functionality (White *et al.* 1994). However, fire planning and fuel reduction projects can move faster (Sturtevant and Jakes 2003).

Focus on Building Relationships and Trust

It is essential to build relationships that create trust. Being inclusive and valuing diversity is a cornerstone of developing trust and building credibility with partners (BLM and Sonoran Institute 2000).

> "The development of trust is something that takes time, and it requires openness, honesty, good communication skills and patience. … Trust is a matter of building credibility and building relationships...and demonstrating an attitude of inclusiveness."
> *(Pipkin and Doerksen 2000, p. 16)*

Trust takes work, especially for collaborations beginning with little common ground. "Yeah, it requires trust—you have to trust each other. That trust doesn't exist when you begin and so that's why you want to talk about goals, you take it a piece at a time" (director, State parks and historic sites department, cited in Belden *et al.* 2001, p. 27).

Successful collaboration starts with the middle ground—the small successes people can agree on—and builds outward. First, it takes the "low-hanging fruit" (Pipkin and Doerksen 2000), starting small and aiming for improvement (USDA 1995). In fuel reduction projects this would be thinning the "small stuff" and clearing around driveways, along roadsides, leaving the big trees, and staying out of contentious areas until trust is built. Also focusing on areas that pose highest risk to communities—these may not be small scale or around driveways and roadsides, but if everyone can agree that they're an imminent threat it builds a lot of good will to work on those right away.

Focus on Strong Leadership

It is essential to have strong leadership. The support of high-level, visible agency or community leaders brings credibility to a collaborative effort, but leaders of collaboration must not fall back on the traditional hierarchical modes of leadership (Chrislip and Larson 1994). Successful collaborations have many leaders with diverse styles and skills: strong, energetic, and motivated leaders who have good communication skills and personal qualities that inspire people (USDA 2000), but also leaders can moderate and facilitate; are inclusive, humble, informative, listeners (USDI 2000); focus on detail; and believe in science (Pipkin and Doerksen 1999). Some successful leaders bring entrepreneurial attitudes (Yaffee and Wondolleck 2000); they are willing to take risks and resolve an impasse in negotiation quickly. Others are ambassadors who can work with a diverse group of stakeholders. Also, new leaders emerge during the process (President's Council on Sustainable Development 1997).

Success is also more likely if individuals in the collaborating group, including agencies, are seen as leaders in the community (Mattessich *et al.* 2001). If community leaders, including those with authority over the issues such as agency managers, are not in the collaboration, they should understand and support the mission of the group (USDA 2000).

" ... [I] t is necessary for them to know they do NOT have all the answers.... The results of effective leadership are dignity, self-reliance and respect for the individuals and communities involved."
(USDA 1995)

Focus on Structure and Process

It is essential to pay attention to the structure of the collaboration and the processes used to conduct business. Successful collaborations are often community-driven (BLM and Sonoran Institute 2000, Cestero 1999), supported by government agency participation. If agencies initiate the partnership, its design should not be predetermined. Stakeholders should be given opportunity to create a structure they believe is fair and inclusive. "The real issue is control of the process—fears of bias based on who initiates the process can be overcome with good facilitation and process design" (Paulson and Chamberlin 1998, p. 4).

Decisionmaking is best regarded if it is transparent and open. "The agencies must constantly be aboveboard and honest—no behind the scenes deals with any party!" (Schuett *et al.* 2001, p. 590). Managers need to be clear early on about their "decision space," the legal "sideboards" (BLM and Sonoran Institute 2000)—laws and regulations that guide public land management.

"The key is to leave the decision-making process in the hands of the community, but not the decision-making authority."
(BLM and Sonoran Institute 2000, p. 7)

Successful collaborative groups are flexible. Participants recognize that not everyone's preferences will be fully met and remain open to different ideas about organization and outcomes (Moote 2003). Being flexible and adaptable allows the group to deal with changing conditions, unique situations, and surprises.

There is no perfect size for a collaborative group, (Paulson and Chamberlin 1998). Some think inclusiveness should take precedence over cohesion of members, and large groups can be managed through subcommittees and spokespersons. Paulson and Chamberlin found that many practitioners had successfully worked with groups of 30-50, and some with groups of more than 200. Optimal group size varies with type and purpose of the collaborative process.

Focus on Outreach and Communication

It is essential to build a strong outreach and communication effort. For fire collaboratives, outreach to homeowners is essential for implementing fuel reduction projects across the landscape. Others' experiences may provide some lessons for accomplishing this step successfully. "Get[ting] involved in the community … helps to build relationships and credibility within the community" (Propst and Rosan 1997, p. 9). Collaborative planning processes create ties and relationships that are strengthened and extended through involvement in the community—offering technical assistance, such as home fire risk audits, or working with local leaders and officials in their planning process (Sturtevant and Jakes 2003).

Successful collaboration requires a strong public outreach and communication effort.

Photo credit: Victoria Sturtevant

Newsletters and multiagency educational workshops are an important form of outreach, especially if the message is clear that it is a joint partnership effort. Collaborators can also make use of opportunities such as festivals, parades, tree planting parties, county fairs (BLM and Sonoran Institute 2000), and similar venues to share their message and hand out informational materials such as fire plans. Outreach can be used not only to inform the public, but also to gather information and bring interested parties on board.

> *Collaborative planning processes create ties and relationships that are strengthened and extended through involvement in the community.*

Focus on Resources

It is essential that important resources be available to the collaboration, including adequate time and consistent funding to support operations and staff. Sixty percent of studies analyzed in one survey (Leach and Pelkey 2001) mentioned the importance of funding and effective leaders, facilitators, or coordinators. Government agencies can be critical players because they are the most likely source of funding (Paulson and Chamberlin 1998), providing staff and meeting space as well. Nonprofit organizations and NGO's also provide an important source of funding, facilitation, and leadership (Sturtevant and Lange 2003, White *et al.* 1994).

Focus on Linkages

It is essential that the collaboration build not only on internal support from local agencies and communities, but also on external support and outside linkages. Successful collaborations integrate regional and national interests (Cestero 1999), addressing concerns of skeptics who believe local decisions sacrifice long-term environmental protection. To connect with information and expertise outside the community, they network with similar community-based groups (Sturtevant and Lange 2003).

Successful agencies create liaison positions; they rethink traditional job descriptions and new administrative structures. Fire agencies could create "cooperative positions" with communities, specialists to work with homeowners. "[The] public doesn't care who he works for, key is that he deals with people who perceive that he works for them ... accessible to people to get help" (Propst and Rosan 1997).

Wildland fire prevention collaboratives need support by the States and communities; Federal agencies do not possess the full range of responsibilities and jurisdictional control to ensure a successful collaboration (Pipkin and Doerksen 2000). Linkages among agencies are also necessary to manage information and standards across boundaries and policies. Agencies have their own systems for classifying and mapping information, which are often not compatible across the landscape (Pipkin and Doerksen 2000); successful collaborations have overcome this problem (Everett 2002).

Focus on Adaptive Management

It is essential that learning comes from reflecting on management decisions and actions—monitoring, reviewing progress, and evaluating the extent to which decisions and actions are accomplishing goals—then adjusting management activities, as necessary. This needs to be a scientifically sound and rigorous process—stakes are often high for collaborators. Pipkin and Doerksen (2000) provide a thorough discussion of adaptive management in collaboration, which will be addressed in this synthesis in appendix B.

Focus on Successes

It is essential to celebrate successes, even small ones, to maintain group motivation, involvement, and focus (Rolle 2002). Early on, the successful collaboration finds tangible outcomes to rally behind and present to others as potential models. Some remind themselves of the intangible outcomes (Carr *et al.* 1998), such as new relationships and the satisfaction of having their neighborhood prepared for an emergency.

"Develop your message, give tours, brag about your partnership." (TNC 2003, p. 5)

Successful pilot projects tend to spread (White *et al.* 1994). A pilot fire project on one property may appeal to neighbors previously unsupportive of fuel reduction recommended by a collaboration (Everett 2002). A pilot fuel reduction effort in one watershed can be used as a model for others, as can collaboratively produced fire-planning documents.

There are many additional lessons to be learned from groups with experience in building and maintaining collaborative processes for wildland fire management. In the following pages we share success stories from nine groups that work collaboratively to manage fuels in their communities.

Four Corners Sustainable Forests Partnership

http://www.rmrs.nau.edu/fourcornersforests/related_links.htm

The Four Corners Sustainable Forests Partnership (FCSFP) was created in 1998 when the State Foresters of New Mexico, Arizona, Utah, and Colorado organized a diverse group of businesses, organizations, and agencies to address forestry concerns in the region. This group sought congressional funding to address increasing risks of catastrophic fire and insect outbreaks and declining community capacity to address forest restoration and forest management needs. In 1999, Congress requested funding for the partnership through State and Private Forestry's Economic Action Programs. The partnership's five main program areas are

community-based forest restoration demonstration grants; regionwide utilization and marketing technical assistance; public information linking community well-being to ecosystem health; regional education and networking; and a revolving loan fund.

A number of local partnerships are networked through this multi-State organization, among them Catron County Citizens Group and Las Humanas in New Mexico. Two groups highlighted here are the Ruidoso Wildland Urban Interface Group (RWUIG) in New Mexico and the Great Flagstaff Forests Partnership (GFFP) in Arizona.

Photo credit: Four Corners Sustainable Forests Partnership Web site

Indigenous Community Enterprises, a member of the Four Corners Sustainable Forests Partnership, worked with members of the Navajo communities to build contemporary hogans with small diameter material.

Applegate Fire Plan

http://www.grayback.com

Fire is no stranger to the Applegate Valley, with its Mediterranean climate and fire-dependent ecosystem. Its land use includes residential lots, small woodland and hobby farms, industrial forests, and public lands; 70 percent of the watershed is managed by the Forest Service and the Bureau of Land Management. Fire suppression, logging, hydraulic mining, and drought have dramatically changed the composition and structure of the forest, much of which consists of overcrowded young and old stands with high levels of insect damage. The risk of catastrophic fire is compounded by the ever-increasing number of rural residential dwellings surrounded by dense, continuous vegetation in the forest interface.

Residents of the Applegate Watershed display their copies of the Applegate Fire Plan, an effort that is often cited as a model of community-driven collaborative fire management planning.

The Applegate Valley straddles two counties (Jackson and Josephine), is within easy reach of two cities (Medford and Grants Pass), and is made up of a number of small, unincorporated communities. A strong attachment to place unites old-timers, mid-timers, and newcomers, as do extensive informal and organizational networks. The Applegate Partnership has served as a place to find common ground and solutions for nearly 10 years and provided the successful proposal for National Fire Plan funding, as well as the leadership and organizational infrastructure to complete the Applegate Plan in 10 months.

The Applegate Fire Plan was both process and product. The process was community-driven, yet 26 Federal, State, and county agencies contributed their staff expertise and support. For the agencies, the plan solidified a process that had been going on for decades: gathering information, balancing priorities, planning strategies, and cooperating over property lines, but this time in dialog and coordination with one another and community members. No one really knew what they were getting into when they embarked on the planning process; the going was tougher than they imagined, but all are proud of the outcomes.

The process included community outreach and education through meetings, newsletters, potlucks, fieldtrips, and demonstration sites. Agencies with differing missions and cultures generated a single set of hazard risk assessment maps, fuel reduction options, and fire suppression strategies. These were included in the reference guide written by a local professional writer, along with instructions for emergency preparedness and other information, ranging from lists of forest consultants to public agency regulations to where to report a fire. Appraisal from local fire departments helped over 600 homeowners work on their properties with National Fire Plan cost-share funds distributed by the Oregon Department of Forestry. The Bureau of Land Management and private landowners have cooperated in thinning across ownership boundaries, sharing tools such as the Slashbuster.

Lessons from the Applegate

1. Promote diversity and the strength it provides. Everyone brings a different piece to the puzzle.
2. Seek common issues and goals. Shared ownership means shared responsibility.
3. Gather an array of leadership skills. You'll need a taskmaster, a coordinator, a cheerleader, a facilitator, and an ambassador.
4. Work at multiple levels and use multiple strategies for outreach. Ultimately, get to the neighborhood level.
5. Build on existing collaborative relationships. Start with a core group of people with demonstrated success at working across boundaries.

6. Keep a deadline for completion. A tight time frame keeps people at the table.
7. Expect controversy. Although fuel management is not as contentious as a timber sale, some people will be suspicious.
8. Be prepared for lots of work. The investment is worth it in the long run.

Central Oregon Partnerships for Wildfire Risk Reduction Project

http://www.coic.org/CED/copwrr/home.htm

The Central Oregon Partnerships for Wildfire Risk Reduction Project (COPWRR) is a multistakeholder collaboration dedicated to reducing wildfire risk in central Oregon through (1) increasing wildfire fuels treatments in central Oregon, and (2) stimulating market uses for small diameter timber. The COPWRR Advisory Council includes a wide variety of environmental, forest industry, community development, tribal, and interagency partners such as the Deschutes and Ochoco National Forests, the Prineville BLM, The Confederated Tribes of Warm Springs, emergency management agencies, State agencies, the Governor's Economic Revitalization Team, and Central Oregon Intergovernmental Council (COIC). In Phase I, the Advisory Council developed the *COPWRR Strategy Framework*, containing 64 recommendations for achieving project goals, including a menu of potential small diameter products/markets for the region. Phase II (wrapping up in fall 2004) is focused upon developing stable, regionally coordinated small diameter supplies through the Governor Kulongoski-endorsed Coordinated Resource Offering Protocol (CROP) initiative. The core goal of Phase III will be to take the processes and analyses completed in Phases I and II, and the agreements developed in the Oregon Solutions process, and direct them toward implementing private sector and community-based small diameter biomass utilization projects. The COPWRR Project and Advisory Council also serve as a community-based "hub" of networking, facilitating, and communication for wildfire risk reduction projects underway in central Oregon.

One key strategy outlined in the *Strategy Framework* is the development of a stable, sustainable supply of small diameter material. The CROP initiative will—through the development of a regional supply offering protocol—help achieve the necessary predictability and stability of supply to enable businesses to invest in technologies and product development. This supply program

The Central Oregon Partnerships for Wildfire Risk Reduction Project brings together stakeholders to develop market uses for small diameter timber.

Photo credit: COPWRR Web site

proposal is predicated on the principle that ecosystem, fuel treatment, and community objectives should drive the volume and characteristics of supply, which would then determine the characteristics of industrial and technological capacity. CROP was presented as a national benchmark pilot initiative to the USDA Forest Service National Leadership Team and Department of the Interior officials in June 2004, in coordination with the Greater Flagstaff Forest Partnership, the Pinchot Institute for Conservation, and Mater Engineering, Ltd.

Governor Kulongoski designated the COPWRR CROP model as an Oregon Solutions initiative in September 2003. A CROP Initiative Team was then created, composed of individuals with a "stake" in ecosystem restoration, community wildfire risk reduction, and employment/job creation in central Oregon. The team will sign a Declaration of Cooperation (DOC) outlining stakeholder support for the CROP initiative in the fall of 2004. The DOC is only the first step toward initiative implementation, and outlines how public agencies, community groups and stakeholders, COIC, private industry, and others will execute and monitor the initiative for years to come.

Greater Flagstaff Forests Partnership

http://www.gffp.org

The Greater Flagstaff Forests Partnership (GFFP) was formed in 1996, after an extreme wildfire season focused public attention on poor forest health and the high risk of catastrophic wildfire in the ponderosa pine forests surrounding Flagstaff, Arizona. The partnership's founding members included the Forest Service, an environmental organization, and a research institute; as a result, its activities reflect ecological and research goals as well as a desire to reduce the wildfire risk. The GFFP's three primary goals are to (1) restore natural ecosystem structures, function, and composition of ponderosa pine forests; (2) manage forest fuels to reduce the probability of catastrophic fire; and (3) research, test, develop, and demonstrate key ecological, economic, and social dimensions of restoration efforts.

The Greater Flagstaff Forests Partnership supports projects that it hopes will reduce the risk of catastrophic fires such as the 1996 Hochderferr Fire.

Photo credit: Greater Flagstaff Forests Partnership Web site

GFFP partners include 27 environmental, research, and governmental organizations. Formally, the partnership is a cooperative agreement between the Coconino National Forest and the Greater Flagstaff Forests Partnership, Inc., a private, nonprofit corporation that serves as a formal advisory committee to the Forest Service under the Federal Advisory Committee Act. In addition to making restoration recommendations to the Forest Service, the GFFP determines the work needed to carry out agreed-on restoration efforts and helps bring financial and human resources to carry out restoration activities. The Forest Service retains all responsibility for developing potential restoration prescriptions, managing the NEPA process and public involvement on proposed restoration projects, and administering all contracts for activities on national forest land. Activities and partnership administration are coordinated by a paid staff and the Coconino National Forest's Community Forestry Liaison.

The GFFP, through its Project Management Team and Multiparty Monitoring Team, has tested over 20 different fuels reduction and restoration prescriptions involving a variety of mechanical thinning techniques and prescribed fire; increasingly, these are focused at the landscape scale. The partnership's first landscape-scale project, the Fort Valley Ecosystem Restoration Project, used several different prescriptions to treat 5,900 acres in a 9,100-acre analysis area. The Kachina Village Forest Health Project includes approximately 12,000 acres, and the

Woody Ridge Project study area includes approximately 30,000 acres. The partnership monitors all of its restoration projects, and project partners are conducting ecological research on several of them.

Because restoration and fuels reduction activities in this region are limited by the lack of forest industry, the GFFP's Utilization and Economic Team (UET) has funded a small-diameter wood utilization study, a small log sawmill site assessment, and a preliminary feasibility assessment for a biomass power plant in northern Arizona. The UET also developed an Enterprise Development Fund for Small Diameter Wood Utilization in Greater Flagstaff to promote greater wood utilization and business development related to small diameter timber resources in the region.

The partnership's Public Information Team maintains ongoing educational efforts that, combined with continued wildfire activity in the region, have resulted in widespread public support for forest treatment, including prescribed burns.

The GFFP focuses its efforts on national forest lands within a 180,000-acre area in and around the city of Flagstaff. However, it also works to coordinate Forest Service projects with forest restoration and fuels reduction efforts on city, county, State, and private land in the region. The GFFP worked jointly with the Ponderosa Fire Advisory Council, a 16-member group of emergency and fire prevention agencies operating in the greater Flagstaff region, to develop a Community Wildfire Protection Plan under the Healthy Forests Restoration Act. That plan covers a 940,000-acre area around Flagstaff and surrounding communities at risk from catastrophic wildfire.

The Josephine County Integrated Fire Plan

http://cwch.uoregon.edu/CCWP/JCIFP/Fire%20Plan/fire_plan.htm

In 2002, the Biscuit Fire burned over 500,000 acres in southern Oregon and California and awakened the rural population, putting over 15,000 citizens on evacuation notice. Although the fire resulted in minimal loss of life and property loss, the costs of suppressing the fire (and the long-term recovery efforts) have exceeded $150 million. This fire helped the Josephine County Board of County Commissioners recognize the need to address the wildfire risk. The commissioners directed the county to develop a countywide fire plan to identify and prioritize communities at risk and hazardous fuels treatment projects, increase public awareness about wildfire risk, and strengthen emergency management procedures during a wildfire.

In 2003, Josephine County contracted with the Program for Watershed and Community Health at the University of Oregon to develop a fire plan. Integration quickly became the focus of the plan as the county and core-planning team recognized the complex set of issues and

In initiating the Josephine County Integrated Fire Plan, planners recognized the need to bring together diverse partners to identify and prioritize projects to reduce fire risk.

Photo credit: Neil Benson

stakeholders. Many citizens live in or move to Josephine County because of the beauty of the forest and its geographic isolation. With the rural population making up over 50 percent of the county's citizens, the need to address fuels conditions on private and adjacent public lands was paramount. The Josephine County Integrated Fire Plan (JCIFP) focused on establishing a collaborative process so that the needs of rural residents would be heard by land management agencies. Likewise, the JCIFP has resulted in opportunities for citizens to learn more about the public agency goals for fire planning and fuels reduction through this process. From the beginning, it was important to find credible, local organizations to partner with throughout the county. Rural fire protection districts, community-based organizations, and social service agencies provided connections to diverse residents and helped established a foundation of trust with community members.

The JCIFP is now a strong partnership among public agencies, fire districts, community-based organizations and citizens. Since its start, the JCIFP has fostered a collaborative environment between its partners to identify and prioritize measures in reducing wildfire risk. The planning process has emphasized a cooperative approach to identify and reach common objectives around fire prevention, education, fuels treatment and other fire-related programs. Goals of the JCIFP include collaborative decisionmaking, providing opportunities for citizen participation, and implementing landscape-scale fuels treatment projects across private and public land boundaries. The JCIFP has also focused on extending resources and opportunities to low-income and other special needs citizens in the county (a significant percentage of the county's population at risk to wildfire.) The primary challenges have been related to the lack of resources in the fire districts and community organizations that would otherwise allow them to be greater participants in the planning and implementation of the JCIFP. JCIFP partners have approached this challenge by dedicating time and energy to providing on-site technical assistance to lower capacity communities.

Orleans/Somes Bar Fire Safe Council

http://www.co.humboldt.ca.us/planning/fire_safe_council/fsc_memb.asp

The Karuk Tribal members, whose ancestral territory includes the area of Orleans and Somes Bar of northern California, were controlling fire long before the Federal government existed. One example is a yearly ritual around Offield Mountain, near present-day Somes Bar, where the tribe rolled flaming logs down the mountainside during a lull in the rainy season, spreading low-intensity ground fire through wide swaths of grasses and understory before the logs were extinguished in the creeks below. Outlawing Native burning practices along with fire suppression has removed a critical ecological process and destroyed a central part of this Native American culture.

The communities of Orleans and Somes Bar are in a unique geographical area. Perhaps more than any other region in California, there is an opportunity for wildland fire use on a scale large enough to restore the area's historic fire regimes. The large expanses of unsettled forest lands surrounding these areas could act as a safety buffer to mitigate the related environmental and

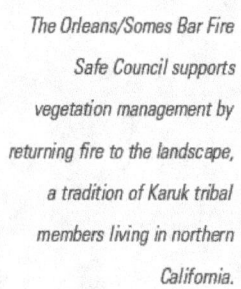

The Orleans/Somes Bar Fire Safe Council supports vegetation management by returning fire to the landscape, a tradition of Karuk tribal members living in northern California.

Photo credit: Orleans/Somes Bar Fire Safe Council Web site

air quality impacts of such a large program. As Karuk Tribal members have known since time immemorial, there now is a realization among non-Native people that fire cannot be excluded from the landscape, and is in fact one of the most powerful land management tools.

Since May of 2001 the Orleans/Somes Bar Fire Safe Council (OSB FSC) has been working to make the mountain communities of Orleans and Somes Bar, in the Mid Klamath Sub-basin of far northern California, resilient to uncharacteristically intense fires that occur with some frequency. With large tracts of wilderness and fire-prone national forests surrounding landowners in all directions, virtually every landowner is in the wildland-urban interface. The OSB FSC is made up of residents from the communities and the Orleans Volunteer Fire Department. Cooperating agencies include Six Rivers National Forest, Klamath National Forest, Humboldt County California Department of Forestry (CDF), Siskiyou County CDF, National Marine Fisheries Service, and the U.S. Fish &Wildlife Service. The Karuk Tribe and OSB FSC are partners; the first OSB FSC grant was coordinated through the tribe and the tribe's fuels reduction crew can work on public lands.

The Orleans/Somes Bar Fire Safe Council adopted the philosophy that managing instead of suppressing fire can provide and foster culturally significant resources, reintroduce natural fire regimes while protecting homes, support wildlife habitat, enhance forest resources, reduce global air quality impacts, and lower fire suppression costs. The Karuk Tribe has the philosophy that the management strategy needed is like managing "into the mirror" (working backwards with a widening view). When you look into a mirror, the first thing you see is yourself. Then you can widen your view and look past yourself to see what you need to do to enhance the ever expanding multitude of resources and ecological processes. These two philosophies took form in 2002. In 2002 the OSB FSC, cleared and set up fuel breaks over 100 strategic acres, using $154,000 in funding from several State and Federal agencies. The OSB FSC employed 20 seasonal workers at wages from $10 to $16 per hour, logged 850 volunteer hours, and held monthly meetings for citizens, environmentalists, and agency representatives to work out details and disputes. In 2003, thinning was completed on another 200 + acres around the Ishi Pishi Road, Orleans, and other private inholdings.

The Southwest Interface Project of Central California

http://www.fs.fed.us/r5/stanislaus/groveland/swift/

The program of work developed by members of SWIFT focuses on creating and maintaining fuelbreaks that protect key watersheds, communities, and significant recreational and other forest resources.

Photo credit: SWIFT Web site

Communities on the slopes of the Sierra Nevada west of Yosemite National Park have seen frequent large fires causing increasingly serious losses of property and other high-value resources and, more significantly, loss of firefighters, lives. In 1999, fire protection and land management agencies in California's southern Tuolumne and northern Mariposa Counties met to identify ways to mitigate the extreme fire dangers in the region. Participants represented two Fire Protection Units of the California Department of Forestry (CDF), two county fire departments, two Resource Conservation agencies with USDA, the USDA Forest Service (Forest Service), USDI Bureau of Land Management (BLM), and the City and County of San Francisco. They referred to themselves as the Southwest Interface Team, or SWIFT. One of their first self-assigned tasks was to map 132,000 acres that include key watersheds providing water and hydroelectric supply to millions of residents, 10 communities and residential concentrations, and significant recreation and forest resources for which all the members share some protection responsibilities.

The team also outlined a program of work emphasizing strategic fire defense systems and pre-fire management planning.

The program of work for strategic fire defense focuses on completing three high priority fuelbreaks. The 2003-2004 SWIFT Program of Work (SWIFT 2003) illustrates how team members fulfill responsibilities for fuelbreak construction and management in different sections of each fuelbreak. For example, in the Bandarita Extension of the Ponderosa Fuelbreak, the Forest Service is responsible for completing an existing contract for shredding fuel material. Agency staff are also responsible for identifying potential and existing helispots and road maintenance needs. The CDF and Mariposa County Fire Department are to work with landowners to determine treatment options on private property. In the Moccasin Extension, the BLM is responsible for determining the need for a water source, helispots, staging areas, and safety zones. The CDF, Tuolumne County Fire Department, and City and County of San Francisco are responsible for identifying private landowners, and starting to secure the rights to cross private lands to accomplish work.

The pre-fire planning work being undertaken by SWIFT is primarily focused on obtaining and displaying information that is critical to maximizing both public and emergency service personnel safety. In writing the strategic plan, political and jurisdictional boundaries were "erased" to develop a plan that meets all local, county, State, and Federal emergency demands.

SWIFT has worked with the public primarily through two local Fire Safe Councils. A Student Conservation Corps team has helped in community outreach. Public officials, local businesses, service organizations, residents and property owners, and other agencies in the area also provide critical support to the project.

SWIFT has documented some lessons it has learned over the past 5 years on the process of collaboration:

1. Identify the project objective and locate the project area on a map.
2. Identify what agencies should be involved.
3. Select your participants—it's important to have field-oriented representatives who are able to make appropriate agency-level decisions on all matters pertaining to accomplishing the project objectives.
4. Develop a team of leaders with a strong sense of commitment and dedication.
5. Obtain line officer/manager support and keep them informed.
6. Become a formal organization early in the process—develop Memorandums of Understanding, county resolutions, communication plans; set formal monthly meetings (with agendas and objectives); and assign a coordinator.
7. Don't let political, administrative, or jurisdictional boundaries conflict with meeting the project objectives.
8. Show results before soliciting public support and participation.
9. It takes time and effort to be successful—the right people with the right support can make it happen.

Wallowa Resources

http://www.wallowaresources.org/

Working with diverse partners, Wallowa Resources supports projects that benefit the local ecology and economy, including projects for research, monitoring, and assessment.

Photo credit: Wallowa Resources Web site

In a community where in the early 1990s environmentalists were hanged in effigy, drivers of green trucks did not receive waves, and three sawmills closed due to declining timber harvests on public lands, a group of people met around a table in the back room of the local bakery to make peace. The table expanded as people became committed to new relationships and solutions and found a common goal: to blend ecological needs of the land with economic needs of the community, preserving the area's rural way of life for future generations. In 1996 Wallowa Resources was formed, a nonprofit group providing leadership to meet these goals; in 1999 it became one of the first groups in the nation to sign a Memorandum of Understanding with the USDA Forest Service committing both parties "to work cooperatively to demonstrate new watershed management approaches that improve and restore the ecosystem health of the Wallowa-Whitman National Forest."

Wallowa Resources believes the future of its rural community rests on a strong restoration economy and a new culture of stewardship that encourages various interest groups to build relationships on principles of transparency, inclusivity, and democracy. The restoration work of Wallowa Resources' started with small-scale improvements and non-controversial issues; with each success, projects expanded. Assessment and monitoring, whose scientific quality is ensured by external partners, are central to these programs.

Today, working with key agencies and private citizens, and funded by private foundations and Federal contracts, Wallowa Resources is making a difference in the long-term economic and ecological health of Wallowa County. Community Smallwood Solutions, a for-profit arm of the organization, adds value to small diameter logs with roundwood products, including untreated Douglas-fir posts and poles for organic vineyards and habitat enhancement and watershed restoration products for Forest Concepts LLC. With the help of a local log home company and the Forest Products Laboratory in Wisconsin, they have built small diameter structures such as the roundwood kiosk that served as an information center at the 2002 Winter Olympics.

Past timber management practices and fire exclusion in Wallowa County have contributed to the buildup of fuels and crowding out of early serial species (e.g., ponderosa pine and western larch). This fuel density, simplification of stand structure, and shift in species composition increase the probability of large-fire, insect, and disease disturbances. Between 1986 and 1996, five catastrophic wildfires occurred, compared to two much smaller events in the previous years. Current assessments rank the risk of catastrophic fire as high. Working with diverse partners, Wallowa Resources helped organize a project to reduce the risk of catastrophic fire to private property around Wallowa Lake. This project increased the skills of local contractors who continue to provide this service to other private landowners in the area; a current project involves about 100 landowners.

Ruidoso Wildland Urban Interface Group

http://www.voruidoso.com/CFMP.html

In New Mexico, concern over wildfire danger was keen even before the New Mexico State Forestry Division listed Ruidosa at the top of the State's 20 most vulnerable interface communities (the USDA Forest Service rated Ruidoso second in the U.S.). In Ruidoso, local collaboration to conduct wildfire mitigation over a broad area might be described as "integrative utilization," whereby each partner contributes some component—from stump to consumer—to the overall mechanism of community forestry. The approach reflects broader regional efforts to organize a multiparty/agency program to rebuild a community-based forest products economy that works to improve forest health, as well as provide wildfire protection. Toward this end, Ruidoso wears "two hats," says Village Forester, Rick DeIaco: one for the Ruidoso Community Fire Management Plan on private and municipal land within village limits; the other for the "Wildland-Urban Interface Working Group," a community-based partnership working on the "Eagle Creek Fuels Reduction Project" upstream on Lincoln National Forest land in the town's watershed.

The Ruidoso Wildland Urban Interface Group not only works with private landowners, so also builds partnerships with public managers who are responsible for fuels treatment on land within the community's watershed.

Local, county, State, and Federal governments and agencies make up the WUI partnership. It has been funded by National Fire Plan dollars made available through the Western Wildland Urban Interface Grants Program. The goal has been to create a buffer on public and tribal land adjacent to the village, to lessen crown-fire potential, and force fires to the ground before they reach residential areas. The in-village ordinance aims to trim "ladder" fuels that could carry flames into the forest canopy. Upstream in the village's watershed, more substantial wildfire mitigation and forest restoration is taking place through the Eagle Creek Fuels Reduction Project.

Similar activities occur on both projects: the village transports homeowners' green waste (with grapple-hook trucks) to dumpsters provided by Sierra Contracting composters. On public land, another partner, Sherry Barrow Strategies, Inc., manufactures the green small-diameter timber into animal bed shavings. Like Sierra Contracting, SBS, Inc. is another entrepreneurial achievement integrating the economic model into a multiparty partnership effort that uses a variety of public and private funding.

"The service and outreach program has expanded far beyond what we expected," DeIaco said. "The first year we hauled 20,000 cubic yards away, last year it was 40,000, and this year we are expecting 60,000."

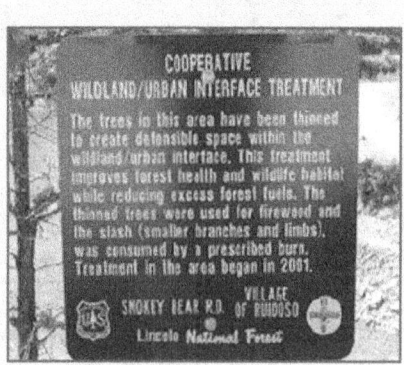

Photo credit: Village of Ruidoso Web site

Acknowledgements

The authors would like to thank the following people who made significant contributions to the content of this document: Kathie Detmar, Colorado State University; Kimberly Harding, Ecological Restoration Institute; and Corinne Corson, private consultant. Adeline and Monica Rother searched literature and contributed annotations to the bibliography. The authors would also like to thank Sarah McCaffrey, USDA Forest Service, North Central Research Station, and three anonymous reviewers for their valuable suggestions for improving the manuscript.

Photo credit: Pamela Jakes

Collaboration between communities, forest managers, and local industries can encourage the use of small-diameter trees removed during fuels treatment projects for unique products like this wooden office divider.

Appendix A—Types of Collaboration

Although collaborative groups seldom identify themselves according to academic categories, it is useful to investigate different types of collaboration to illustrate the variety of structures and organizations that work collaboratively. A discussion of the types of collaboration can also help managers, citizens, and others identify the role they might play in these groups. Three different approaches to categorizing collaboratives are discussed below: categorization by the strength of the linkages between members, by the focus or scale of the projects, and by the membership in the collaborative.

Collaboration Characterized by the Strength of Linkages

Mandell (1999a) described a range of associations between individuals and groups that can be considered collaborations. For each we offer examples from the wildland fire prevention and fuels mitigation literature to help illustrate that type.

Informal linkages or interactive contacts between two or more organizations are the most basic type of collaboration. The Lomakatsi Restoration Project in the Rogue River Basin of Oregon works collaboratively with private landowners to create fuel reduction projects that are a "holistic, ecological example of 'true restoration'" (Lomakatsi Restoration Project 2002). Some Federal agency staff maintain informal contact with members of the project, referring local residents hesitant to undertake fuel reduction to the project because of its "soft touch" management approach (Sturtevant and Corson 2003).

A second type of cooperation is characterized by two or more organizations that coordinate intermittently or adjust their policies to accomplish an objective. An example of this type would be the cooperation that exists between the Medford District of the BLM and residents of Jackson County, Oregon. The district and area residents work together to complete fuels reduction projects on Federal lands adjacent to private property. BLM also coordinates the use of the slashbuster (a tractor mounted, mechanical device that shreds woody vegetation), employing it across ownership boundaries to reduce fuels (Sturtevant and Jakes 2003).

A third type of collaboration is the ad hoc or temporary task force that organizes to accomplish a purpose or purposes. In Bend, Oregon, local, State and Federal fire managers and a community group formed a task force to convince county officials to allocate funding for a reverse 911 phone system. This system is used to reach residents during wildland fire emergencies (Sturtevant and Jakes 2003).

A fourth type of collaboration is partnerships that encourage the permanent or regular coordination between individuals and groups through formal agreements to engage in limited activity to achieve a purpose or purposes. In Ashland, Oregon, four non-industrial private landowners, the City, Forest

Service, a land trust organization, and a private consulting forester developed the Hamilton Creek Coordinated Resource Management Plan (CRMP), a nonbinding agreement describing how their shared watershed should use thinning and fire-safe home construction materials to mitigate fire risk (Main 1996).

A fifth type of collaboration is coalitions. Coalitions generally have a fairly narrow purpose or scope, and members take independent actions that are planned sequentially or simultaneously with other members. In Roslyn, Washington, Forest Service and Washington Department of Natural Resource fire managers have worked with local schools to develop a Jr. Firewise program, The activities of this program culminate with students burning their model houses to evaluate the success of their "defensible space" (Kruger and Sturtevant 2004).

The final type of collaboration are collaborative groups. We defined collaboration earlier, but Mandall's characterization of a collaborative group is as collective networks or structures

> *A discussion of the types of collaboration can also help managers, citizens, and others identify the role they might play in these groups.*

with a broad mission that is accomplished by members undertaking joint and/or strategically integrated independent action. The structural arrangement allows the collaborative to take on broad tasks that reach beyond the abilities or authorities of the independently operating organizations. An example of a collaborative involved in fuels management is the National Fire Plan Implementation Team (NFPIT) in Silver City, New Mexico. Composed of many agencies and organizations with differing sets of responsibilities for wildland fire issues, NFPIT is a community-driven effort to develop strategies and projects such as wildland fire planning, forest restoration, fuels reduction, public outreach, and economic development (Steelman and Kunkel 2003).

Collaboration Characterized by the Focus or Scale of the Project

Mandell's (1999a) continuum of collaboration focuses the linkages between members of the collaborative. Cestero (1999) offers an alternative classification scheme based on whether the association is focused on activities that are (1) place- and project-based or (2) policy-based.

Place- or project-based collaboratives are initiated by local, volunteer leaders respected by a spectrum of local residents. Participants are involved as individuals, representing their own interests and concerns rather than their specific constituencies or interest groups. Many of these groups use consensus-building, dialog, and collaborative learning to build relationships and trust and to foster stewardship. They provide forums for the geographic community to share knowledge and values on land management issues, and undertake projects across boundaries. Place- or project-based collaboratives are perceived as producing more civil dialog and resulting in on-the-ground conservation benefits (Cestero 1999). Groups such as local Firewise committees are examples of place-based initiatives.

Policy-based collaboratives are generally focused on regional or national resource policy issues. They are often made up of associations with a strong stake in the outcome of the decisions and therefore are generally less inclusive of local leaders and residents (Cestero 1999). Because of their policy focus, this type of collaborative produces fewer on-the ground benefits. The Western Governors' Association is an example of a policy-based collaborative that focuses on wildfire issues at the regional level.

Collaboration Characterized by Membership

Collaboration has also been classified according to member composition: citizen-based, agency-based, and mixed partnerships (Moore and Koontz 2003). In addition to any on-the-ground projects, citizen-based groups often engage in activities such as lobbying and petitioning. They often report their accomplishments as increased public awareness and policy influence (Moore and Koontz 2003). Local Fire Safe Councils and the many watershed conservation groups would be examples of citizen-based collaboratives.

Mixed and agency-based groups are more focused on planning, building relationships, and problem solving. For accomplishments they tend to report the development of management plans, group development and sustainability, and increased public awareness (Moore and Koontz 2003). An example of a mixed collaborative group would be the SouthWest InterFace Team (SWIFT) in central California. In this collaborative, Federal, State, county, and city agencies, conservation groups, and Fire Safe Councils come together to implement projects that will mitigate the extreme wildfire problems in the area (SWIFT 2003). NIFC would be a classic example of an agency-based collaborative.

Appendix B—Monitoring and Evaluation

Kimberly Harding and Ann Moote, Ecological Restoration Institute

Why Evaluate Collaboration?

In 2001, the National Academy of Public Administration called for increased program evaluation to "support strategic planning and performance management for [coordinated fire management] and to evaluate the efficiency, effectiveness, and efficacy of Fire Policy and National Fire Plan activities" (Fairbanks *et al.* 2001, p. xxvii).

Well-designed monitoring and evaluation provides a means for determining how effective collaboration has been. Naturally, collaborative group efforts will be treated seriously only if they prove themselves to work (Provan and Milward 2001). Monitoring and evaluation gives the collaborative group an opportunity to assess its effectiveness and improve its accountability—which in turn can improve trust both among collaborative group participants and those outside of the process. Participants, community members, academics, policymakers, facilitators, critics, agencies, and those who provide funding all have an interest in the outcome of the collaborative group effort (Conley and Moote 2003).

From the perspective of those who are considering engaging in collaboration, the two main reasons for monitoring and evaluating the effort may be time and money. Through the monitoring and evaluation process, those involved in the collaborative group will better understand if their investment of energy results in a positive product and can determine if their efforts need to be refined to efficiently meet the group's objectives. Nonparticipants may be more likely to contribute if they see that their time will benefit their community (Susskind *et al.* 1999).

> *Monitoring and evaluation gives the collaborative group an opportunity to assess its effectiveness and improve its accountability—which in turn can improve trust both among collaborative group participants and those outside of the process.*

Furthermore, evaluation provides funders with an explanation of the risks associated with donating money to the collaborative effort (Leach *et al.* 2002).

Who Should Evaluate?

Determining who will perform the monitoring and evaluation may be constrained by time, money, and participant expertise. Many groups favor self-evaluation. However, to ensure good sampling design and reduce bias, it has been advised that collaborative groups hire a trained researcher or evaluator from a university, consulting firm, or government agency. When the primary goal is to evaluate the group itself, collaborative groups should also consider hiring an evaluator that is not involved with the group or connected to the issue (Susskind *et al.* 1999). This may be difficult for groups who are constrained by funding; however, in a study performed by the GAO (2003), where five Federal agencies were assessed for the capacity to perform evaluations, results indicated that creative methods for leveraging funds are available.

How to Evaluate?

Five important guidelines should be considered when designing a monitoring or evaluation protocol (GAO 1991):

- Ask the right questions,
- State the question in the right way,
- Focus on the group's objectives (short term and long term),
- Design the evaluation appropriately (e.g., do not use an extensively long evaluation for a small group or simple problem), and
- Consider the specific constraints as related to executing the evaluation (e.g., time, cost, staff expertise, location, and facilities).

Depending on the goals, the monitoring or evaluation questions asked may address implementation (did the group do what it said it would do?), effectiveness (did the group achieve its goals?), or validation (did the actions taken have the expected outcomes?) (Ecological Restoration Institute *et al.* 2003). When asking participants or outside observers to assess a process or its outcomes, evaluators should consider using a combination of descriptive, normative, and impact questions. Questions of a descriptive nature measure what people think and how they feel about the group's process or outcome. Normative questions focus on "what should have been," instead of "what was." Impact questions address the observed outcomes of the process (GAO 1991). All of these types of questions can be implemented

All of these types of questions can be implemented through a variety of evaluation designs, including sample surveys, case studies, field experiments, and use of existing data.

through a variety of evaluation designs, including sample surveys, case studies, field experiments, and use of existing data (GAO 1991).

Survey and Sampling Design

Provan and Milward (2001) recommended evaluating a collaborative effort from three different perspectives to determine how it has affected (1) the environment and the community, (2) the collaborative group itself, and (3) the organizations that are participating in the effort. Based on their survey of 770 participants from 44 different collaborative watershed groups, Leach *et al.* (2002) warned that it is important to get a good cross section of respondents, including nonparticipants as well as participants. In their study, group coordinators tended to report higher rates of success and participants tended to be more polarized (either more positive or more negative) than nonparticipants.

Baseline Data

It can be difficult to make claims beyond the very concrete accomplishments of a project. Yet, to justify the project—and to receive public and private support—collaborative groups often need to show some degree of causality, or illustrate the project caused the changes being measured. Unless good baseline data have been collected and clear information has been recorded on the results of the project, using accurately measured variables in the same manner during the course of the project, it is difficult to defend a project or management practice or give reasons why an effort should be expanded (Ecological Restoration Institute *et al.* 2003).

Timing

Monitoring and evaluation should be conducted throughout the course of the collaborative effort to determine whether progress is being made toward the group's original goal. This allows the group to evaluate the effectiveness of its methods and adjust them if necessary. Measurements taken some time after the project has been implemented allow assessment of longer term effects.

What to Measure?

There is no standard set of criteria and indicators for monitoring a project or evaluating its effectiveness. The collaborative group's interests, the type of effort being assessed, and the values of those conducting the assessment will all play a role in determining what to measure (Conley and Moote 2003).

Some research suggests that evaluating a collaborative group's process (e.g., communication mechanisms, ability to reach decisions) is most useful (e.g., Buckle and Buckle-Thomas 1986). However, in terms of collaborative resource management, there is an increased focus on evaluating outcomes (Kenney 2000, Leach *et al.* 2002). Most researchers recommend evaluating a collaborative group's efforts against its stated goals, although some may also want to determine whether the fears or expectations of participants or observers have been realized.

Improved environmental outcomes are typically the primary goal for many participants in, and observers of, collaborative conservation groups. Determining environmental changes resulting from group decisions and activities is difficult, however, because it requires good baseline data and careful elimination of external causal factors (e.g., climate change, flood event). Furthermore, environmental impacts may not be evident for several years after a management action has been implemented. Because of these challenges, researchers frequently use intermediate indicators, such as numbers of restoration projects implemented or changed management practices, to evaluate environmental outcomes (Born and Genskow 2000, Imperial and Hennessey 2000, Leach *et al.* 2002). Evaluators should acknowledge the limitations of intermediate indicators, however: the fact that a restoration project was implemented does not necessarily mean that it will result in the desired effects on the environment. Good intermediate indicators are those that evaluators and stakeholders agree are expected to result in desired outcomes.

Kenney (2000) outlined broad indicators of both process and outcome success that may be applicable to many collaborative groups:
- Improved health to the natural resource,
- Improved trust between stakeholders and partners,
- Increased communication between parties,
- Expansion of the decisionmaking capacity,
- Implementation of new decisionmaking processes, and
- Implementation of new management and planning processes.

In a document evaluating progress of the Applegate Partnership, Rolle (2002) addressed three main questions that have benefited this collaborative group:
- How well does the group meet its own mission?
- Did the group achieve the desired outcome?
- Has there been appreciable movement toward meeting the desired results?

Once the group has identified the questions it wants to answer, it must select one or more specific indicators that can be used to measure change in that area. An indicator is a unit of information measured over time that documents changes in a specific condition. A good indicator meets the criteria of being measurable, precise, consistent, and sensitive. When selecting indicators, multiparty monitoring groups will want to ask themselves whether a proposed indicator is:
- Relevant for the site and treatment,
- Sensitive enough to detect change within a specific timeframe,
- Defensible and not subject to individual or organized bias, and
- Able to be measured by methods that are professionally accepted and understood (Ecological Restoration Institute *et al.* 2003).

For example, if a group has decided that one of its goals is to reduce the risk of catastrophic wildland fire, it may select percent tree canopy closure as an indicator. Or, if the group has chosen to monitor quality of life in the community, it may select employment conditions in restoration-related industries as the indicator, which might be measured in terms of average wages in restoration-related jobs or by the number of restoration workers who receive health benefits from their employer (Ecological Restoration Institute *et al.* 2003).

> *Improved environmental outcomes are typically the primary goal for many participants in, and observers of, collaborative conservation groups.*

Appendix C—Partnering Mechanisms in the USDA Forest Service

The Forest Service Manual contains a number of mechanisms for collaborating with other agencies, businesses, nonprofit groups, and communities (Loucks 2002). These include:

- Challenge Cost-Share Agreements (FSM 1587.12)
- Collection Agreements (FSM 1584)
- Cooperative Agreements (FSM 1581)
- Cooperative Fires Protection Agreements (FSM 1582)
- Cooperative Law Enforcement Agreements (FSM 1582)
- Cooperative Research and Development Agreements (FSM 1587.14)
- Cooperative Forest Road Agreements (FSM 1582)
- Grants (FSM 1582)
- Interagency and Intra-agency Agreements (FSM 1585)
- Memoranda of Understanding (FSM 1586)
- Letters of Intent (FSM 1586)
- Participating Agreements (FSM 1587.11)
- Joint Venture Agreements (FSM 1587.13)
- Cost-Reimbursable Agreements (FSM 1587.13)

Appendix D—The Federal Advisory Committee Act (FACA)

FACA was originally created to (1) reduce what was considered to be an excessive number of committees advising Federal agencies and (2) reduce bias within advisory committees by requiring them to be open and broadly representative. Unanticipated results of the act have emerged in its implementation.

Advisory committees regulated by FACA must be chartered, and their charter must include details such as the group's scope, a description of duties, and the estimated number and frequency of meetings (Norris-York 1996). The chartering process can take several months, and a charter will be approved only if the advisory committee is "essential to the conduct of agency business and in the public interest" and has "fairly balanced membership" (NRLC 1998). U.S. Department of Agriculture regulations interpreting FACA add other steps to the chartering process, making it even more laborious and time-consuming (USDA 2000). Once chartered, notice of all committee meetings must be published 15 days in advance in the Federal Register, including time, date, place, and agenda. Public access to Federal advisory committee meetings is mandatory and detailed minutes must be kept (Norris-York 1996). In addition, a designated Federal employee must attend each meeting (NRLC 2000).

> *U.S. Department of Agriculture regulations interpreting FACA add other steps to the chartering process, making it even more laborious and time-consuming (USDA 2000).*

The most problematic are ambiguous terms in the act that make it unclear when FACA applies and when it does not, and onerous administrative requirements for creating and maintaining advisory committees when the act does apply (Norris-York 1996, NRLC 2000, USDA 2000).

FACA's procedural requirements apply to advisory committees "established by" or "utilized by" a Federal agency to obtain advice or recommendations. Legal experts generally agree that FACA applies to advisory committees established by:

1. Federal statute or reorganization plan,
2. the President, and
3. Federal agencies.

It is also clear that certain groups are explicitly excluded from FACA, including those made up solely of government officials (Federal, tribal, State, or local), recovery plan teams authorized under the

Endangered Species Act, and civic groups that provide public services to FACA-chartered committees (Loucks and Kostishack 2001, NRLC 2000, USDA 2000).

Disputes arise, however, over the term "utilized by" a Federal agency, and this term has sometimes been interpreted to apply to community-based and collaborative associations. According to analysis conducted by the Natural Resources Law Center in the late 1990s, "there are three requirements that must be satisfied in order for a 'utilized' advisory committee to come within the mandates of FACA:
1. there must be a committee,
2. the committee must formulate advice by consensus, and
3. the committee's advice must be 'utilized' by a federal agency" (NRLC 2000).

New regulations created by the General Services Administration in 2001 further clarify that FACA requirements do not apply to groups whose members are not actually managed or controlled by the executive branch, who provide individual advice, or who exchange facts or information, but not advice (USDA 2002).

Collaborative outreach to homeowners is essential for implementation of fuel reduction projects across the landscape.

Photo credit: Victoria Sturtevant

The courts have interpreted the phrase "utilized by" even more narrowly, limiting FACA to groups "organized by, or closely tied to, the Federal Government, and thus enjoying quasi-public status" and stating that agency membership in an advisory group is not sufficient to trigger FACA (NRLC 2000). Based on the case law, some legal scholars have concluded that most community-based and collaborative groups are not subject to FACA (NRLC 2000). Others, however, including some agency lawyers, disagree (Loucks and Kostishack 2001).

Ongoing debates and confusion about FACA have led some Forest Service personnel to believe that FACA forbids them from meeting regularly with any group that does not have a FACA charter and from seeking advice from any nongovernmental group (Loucks and Kostishack 2002, USDA 2000). This "FACA Fear" also stems from the threat that interest groups will use FACA lawsuits to stop government action they oppose for other reasons (Loucks and Kostishack 2001). Although an agency would clearly be violating Federal law if it gave a collaborative group decisionmaking authority over Federal lands management (Coggins 1999), many outside the agency believe that it is overly cautious on this issue:

> At times, the agency's interpretation of FACA is so strict as to lead partners to believe that it is being used by Federal agencies to thwart collaborative activities that they wish to avoid for other reasons (Loucks and Kostishack 2001, p. 8).

The Forest Service has asked its Collaboration Team to develop language clarifying this issue. In the meantime, NRLC (2000) advises that collaborative groups structure their meetings around one of the exemptions in the act itself, for example, specifically structuring meetings so that only information and not advice is exchanged. Section 102 of the Healthy Forests Restoration Act states that "the Federal Advisory Committee Act … shall not apply to the planning process and recommendations concerning community wildfire protection plans."

Literature Cited

Arganoff, Robert; McGuire, Michael. 1999. *Managing in network settings.* Policy Studies Review. 16(1): 18-41.

Aspen Institute: Rural Economic Policy Program. 1996. *Measuring community capacity building: a workbook in progress for rural communities.* Aspen, CO: The Aspen Institute: 3-96. [Available only on internet: http://www.aspeninstitute.org/bookdetails.asp?i=&d=60].

Baker, Mark; Kusel, Jonathan. 2003. *Community forestry in the United States: learning from the past, crafting the future.* Covelo, CA: Island Press. 247 p.

Beaulieu, Lionel J. 2002. *Mapping the assets of your community: a key component for building local capacity.* SRDC Publ. 227. Mississippi State, MS: Mississippi State University: Southern Rural Development Center. http://srdc.msstate.edu

Belden Russonello; Stewart Research and Communications. 2001. *Collaborative process: better outcomes for all of us: communications recommendations and analysis of 54 interviews with decision makers on environmental issues in the Western U.S.* Washington, DC: The Emily Hall Tremaine Foundation and Partners. 36 p. http://www.merid.org/PDF/BRS_Report.pdf

Bentrup, Gary. 2001. *Evaluation of a collaborative model: a case study analysis of watershed planning in the intermountain west.* Environmental Management. 27(5): 739-748.

Bernard, Tom; Young, Jora. 1997. *The ecology of hope: communities collaborate for sustainability.* Gabriola Island, BC: New Society Publishers. 233 p.

Birkholz, A.; Lineback, P. 2001. *Technology and collaboration improve interagency fire planning.* Natural Resource Year in Review-2001, U.S. Department of the Interior, National Park Service. [Available only on Internet: http://www2.nature.nps.gov/YearInReview/yir2001/07_collaboration/07_4_birkholz_SEKI.html].

Blahna, Dale J.; Yonts-Shepard, Susan. 1989. *Public involvement in resource planning: toward bridging the gap between policy and implementation.* Society and Natural Resources. 2: 209-227.

Blumberg, Louis. 1999. *Preserving the public trust.* Forum for Applied Research and Public Policy. 14(2): 89-93.

Blumberg, Louis; Knuffke, Darrell. 1998. *Count us out: why the wilderness society opposed the Quincy Library Group legislation.* Chronicle of Community. 2(2): 41-44.

Born, Stephen M.; Genskow, Kenneth D. 2000. *The watershed approach: an empirical assessment of innovation in environmental management.* Res. Pap. 7. Washington, DC: National Academy of Public Administration. 62 p.

Borrini-Feyerabend, Grazia. 1996. *Collaborative management of protected areas: tailoring the approach to the context.* [Available only on Internet: http://www.iucn.org/themes/spgeng/Tailor/TailorNF.html].

Brick, Philip D.; Cawley, R. McGreggor. 1996. *A wolf in the garden: the land rights movement and the new environmental debate.* Lanham, MD: Rowman & Littlefield Publishers. 318 p.

Brick, Philip; Snow, Donald; Van de Wetering, Sarah. 2001. *Across the Great Divide: explorations in collaborative conservation and the American West.* Covelo, CA: Island Press. 286 p.

Britell, Jim. 2003. *Essay #10: partnerships, roundtables and Quincy-type groups are bad ideas that cannot resolve environmental conflicts.* [Available only on Internet: http://www.britell.com/use/uselo.html].

Brunner, Ronald D.; Colburn, Christine H.; Cromley, Christina M.; Klein, Roberta A.; Olson, Elizabeth A. 2002. *Finding common ground: governance and natural resources in the American West.* New Haven, CT: Yale University Press. 303 p.

Buckle, Leonard G.; Thomas-Buckle, Suzann R. 1986. *Placing environmental mediation in context: lessons from 'Failed' mediations.* Environmental Impact Assessment Review. 6: 55-70.

Budd-Falen, Karen. 1996.
Protecting community stability and local economies: opportunities for local government influence in federal decision- and policy-making processes. In: Brick, Philip D.; Cawley, R. McGreggor, eds. A wolf in the garden: the land rights movement and the new environmental debate. Lanham, MD: Rowman & Littlefield Publishers: 73-83.

Burns, Sam; Richard, Tim. 2002.
Four corners sustainable forests partnership 2001-02 demonstration grants program evaluation report. Durango, CO: Fort Lewis College, Office of Community Services. 50 p.

Carr, Deborah S.; Selin, Steven W.; Schuett, Michael A. 1998.
Managing public forests: understanding the role of collaborative planning. Environmental Management. 22(5): 767-776.

Cestero, Barb. 1999.
Beyond the hundredth meeting: a field guide to collaborative conservation on the West's public lands. Tucson, AZ: Sonoran Institute. 80 p.

Chaskin, R.J. 2001.
Building community capacity: A definitional framework and case studies from a comprehensive community initiative. Urban Affairs Review. 36(3): 291-323.

Chaskin, Robert J.; Brown, Prudence; Venkatesh, Sudhir; Vidal, Avis. 2001.
Collaborations, partnerships, and organizational networks. In: Building community capacity. New York, NY: Aldine de Gruyter: 123-157.

Chrislip, D.; Larson, C. 1994.
Collaborative leadership: how citizens and civic leaders can make a difference. San Francisco, CA: Jossey-Bass. 192 p.

Cigler, Beverly A. 1999.
Pre-conditions for the emergence of multi-community collaborative organizations. Policy Studies Review. 16(1): 86-102.

Coggins, George C. 1999.
Regulating federal natural resources: a summary case against devolved collaboration. Ecology Law Quarterly. 25: 602-610.

Coggins, George C. 2001.
Of Californicators, Quislings and Crazies: some perils of devolved collaboration. In: Brick, Philip D.; Snow, D.; Van de Wetering, S.B., eds. Across the Great Divide: explorations in collaborative conservation and the American West. Washington, DC: Island Press: 163-171.

Committee of Scientists. 1999.
Sustaining the people's lands: recommendations for stewardship of the national forests and grasslands into the next century. Washington, DC: U.S. Department of Agriculture, Forest Service; n.p. [Available only on Internet: http://www.fs.fed.us/news/news_archived /science/cosfrnt.pdf].

Conley, Alexander; Moote, Margaret A. 2003.
Evaluating collaborative natural resource management. Society for Natural Resources. 16: 371-386.

Cortner, H.J.; Moote, M.A. 1999.
Collaborative stewardship in action: building a civic society. In: Cortner, H.J.; Moote, M.A., eds. The politics of ecosystem management. Washington, D.C.: Island Press: 91-108.

Coughlin, Christine W.; Hoben, Merrick L.; Manskopf, Dirk W.; Quesada, Shannon W. 1999.
A systematic assessment of collaborative resource management partnerships. Ann Arbor, MI: University of Michigan, School of Natural Resources. [Available only on Internet: http://www.snre.umich.edu/emi/pubs/crmp .htm].

Creighton, James L. 1992.
Involving citizens in community decision making: a guidebook. Washington, DC: Program for Community Problem Solving. 227 p.

Curtis, Allan; Shindler, Bruce; Wright, Angela. 2002.
Sustaining local watershed initiatives: lessons from landcare and watershed councils. Journal of the American Water Resources Association. 38(5): 1207-1216.

Daniels, Steven E.; Walker, Gregg B. 2001.
Working through environmental conflict: the collaborative learning approach. Westport, CT: Praeger. 299 p.

Daniels, Steven E.; Walker, Gregg B.; Carroll, Matthew S.; Blatner, Keith A. 1996.
Using collaborative learning in fire recovery planning. Journal of Forestry. 94(8): 4-9.

Diduck, Alan; Sinclair, A. John. 2002.
Public involvement in environmental assessment: the case of the nonparticipant. Environmental Management. 29(4): 578-588.

Duane, Timothy P. 1997.
Community participation in ecosystem management. Ecology Law Quarterly. 24(4): 771-797.

Dukes, E. Franklin; Firehock, Karen. 2001.
Collaboration: a guide for environmental advocates. Charlottesville, VA: University of Virginia. 70 p.

Ecological Restoration Institute; Forest Trust; Four Corners Institute; National Forest Foundation; Pinchot Institute for Conservation; USDA Forest Service – Collaborative Forest Restoration Program. 2003.
Multiparty monitoring and assessment guidelines for community based forest restoration in Southwestern ponderosa pine forests. Albuquerque, NM: U.S. Department of Agriculture, Forest Service, Collaborative Forest Restoration Program. 109 p.

Ecosystem Management Initiative. n.d.
Collaboration. [Available only on Internet: www.snre.umich.edu/emi/collaboration/definitions.htm].

Everett, Y.
In press. *Community participation in fire management planning: the Trinity County Fire Safe Council's Fire Plan.* In: Narog, M.G., tech. coord. Proceedings of the 2002 Fire Conference on Managing Fire and Fuels in the Remaining Wildlands and Open Spaces of the Southwestern United States; 2002 December 2-5; San Diego, CA. Gen. Tech. Rep. PSW-189. Albany, CA: U.S. Department of Agriculture, Forest Service, Pacific Southwest Research Station.

Fairbanks, Frank; Gardner, Henry; Hill, Elizabeth; Mulrooney, Keith; Philpot, Charles; Weick, Karl; Wise, Charles. 2001.
Managing wildland fire: enhancing capacity to implement the Federal Interagency Policy. Washington, DC: National Academy of Public Administration. 142 p.

FEMAT, Forest Ecosystem Management Assessment Team. 1993.
Forest ecosystem management: an ecological, economic, and social assessment: report of the Forest Ecosystem Management Team. Washington, DC: U.S. Department of Agriculture, Forest Service. Various paging.

Firewise Communities USA. 2003.
Firewise Communities USA Web site. [Available only on Internet: www.firewise.org/usa].

Frentz, Irene C.; Burns, Sam; Voth, Donald E.; Sperry, Charles. 1999.
Rural development and community-based forest planning and management: a new collaborative paradigm. Fayetteville, AR: University of Arkansas. 117 p. plus 114 p. appendices.

Germain, Rene H.; Floyd, Donald W.; Stehman, Stephan V. 2001.
Public perceptions of the USDA Forest Service public participation process. Forest Policy and Economics. 3: 113-124.

Gobster, Paul H.; Hull, R. Bruce. 2000.
Restoring nature: perspectives from the social sciences and humanities. Washington, DC: Island Press. 321 p.

Gray, Barbara. 1985.
Conditions facilitating interorganizational collaboration. Human Relations. 38: 911-936.

Hummel, Mark; Freet, Bruce. 1999.
Collaborative processes for improving land stewardship and sustainability. In: Sexton, W.T.; Malk, A.J.; Szaro, R.C.; Johnson, N.C., eds. Ecological stewardship: a common reference for ecosystem management. Oxford, England: Elsevier Science Ltd. 3(3): 97-129.

Imperial, Mark T.; Hennessey, Timothy. 2000.
Environmental governance in watersheds: the role of collaboration. Bloomington, IN: School of Public and Environmental Affairs, Indiana University. 30 p.

Ingles, Andrew W.; Musch, Arne; Qwist-Hoffmann, Helle. 1999.
The participatory process for supporting collaborative management of natural resources: an overview. Rome, Italy: FAO. 96 p.

KenCairn, Brett. 2000.
Public agencies in collaboration: a panacea to gridlock or the next big debacle? Flagstaff, AZ: Presentation prepared for the national leadership conference, Yale University, October 2000. On file with: U.S. Department of Agriculture, Forest Service, North Central Research Station, 1992 Folwell Avenue, St. Paul, MN 55108. 13 p.

Kenney, Douglas S. 1999.
Are community-based watershed groups really effective? Chronicle of Community. 3(2): 33-37.

Kenney, Douglas S. 2000.
Arguing about consensus: examining the case against western watershed initiatives and other collaborative groups active in natural resources management. Boulder, CO: University of Colorado School of Law, Natural Resources Law Center. 72 p.

Kenney, D.S.; McAllister, S.T.; *et al.* 2000.
The new watershed source book: a directory and review of watershed initiatives in the Western United States. Boulder, CO: University of Colorado School of Law, Natural Resources Law Center. 455 p.

Korfmacher, K.S. 1998.
Invisible successes, visible failures: paradoxes of ecosystem management in the Albermarle-Pamlico Estuarine Study. Coastal Zone Management. 26(3): 191-212.

Kostishack, Peter; Rana, Naureen. 2002.
An introduction to the National Fire Plan: history, structure, and relevance to communities. Washington, DC: Pinchot Institute for Conservation. 55 p.

Kruger, L.; Strutevant, V. 2004.
Roslyn, Washington: steps to improve community preparedness for wildfire. Community Preparedness Case Series: case study #9. 4p.

Kusel, Jonathan; Adler, Elisa. 2003.
Forest communities, community forests: a collection of case studies of community forestry prepared for the seventh American forest congress communities committee. Taylorsville, CA: Forest Community Research. 220 p.

Lange, Jonathon I. 2001.
Exploring paradox in environmental collaborations. In: Brick, Philip D.; Snow, Donald; Van de Wetering, Sandra B., eds. Across the Great Divide: explorations in collaborative conservation and the American West. Washington, DC: Island Press: 200-209.

Leach, William D. 2002.
Surveying diverse stakeholder groups. Society for Natural Resources. 15: 641-649.

Leach, William D.; Pelkey, Neil W. 2001.
Making watershed partnerships work: a review of the empirical literature. Journal of Water Resources Planning and Management. 127(6): 378-385.

Leach, William D.; Pelkey, Neil W.; Sabatier, Paul A. 2002.
Stakeholder partnerships as collaborative policymaking: evaluation criteria applied to watershed management in California and Washington. Journal of Policy Analysis and Management. 21(4): 645-670.

Lee, Kai N. 1993.
Compass and gyroscope: integrating science and politics for the environment. Washington, DC: Island Press. 255 p.

Linden, Russell M. 2002.
Working across boundaries: making collaboration work in government and nonprofit organizations. San Francisco, CA: Jossey-Bass. 302 p.

Lomakatsi Restoration Project. 2002.
Regional Restoration Report. Issue 1. Ashland, OR: Lomakatsi Restoration Project. 12 p.

London, Scott. 1995.
Collaboration and community: a paper prepared for Pew Partnership for Civic Change. [Available only on Internet: http://www.scottlondon.com/reports/ppcc.html].

Loucks, Andrea. 2002.
Strengthening the ties that bind. Washington, DC: The Aspen Institute and Pinchot Institute for Conservation. 28 p.

Loucks, Andrea; Kostishack, Peter. 2001.
Partnership with the USDA Forest Service: improving opportunities and enhancing existing relationships. Acc. No. DP-16-02. Washington, DC: Pinchot Institute for Conservation. 19 p.

Lowrie, Karen W.; Greenberg, Michael R. 2001.
Can David and Goliath get along? Federal land in local places. Environmental Management. 28(6): 703-711.

Machlis, Gary E.; Kaplan, Amanda B.; Tuler, Seth P.; Bagby, Kathleen A.; McKendry, Jean E. 2002.
Burning questions: a social science research plan for federal wildland fire management. Moscow, ID: University of Idaho. n.p.

Main, Martin, L. 1996.
Protection and restoration of a fire-adapted ecosystem in Southwestern Oregon: a case study. Seattle, WA: University of Washington. 92 p. M.S. thesis.

Mandell, Myrna. 1999a.
The impact of collaborative efforts: changing the face of public policy through networks and network structures. Policy Studies Review. 16(1): 4-15.

Mandell, Myrna P. 1999b.
Community collaborations: working through network structures. Policy Studies Review. 16(1): 42-64.

Margerum, Richard D. 1999.
Integrated environmental management: the foundations for successful practice. Environmental Management. 24(2): 151-166.

Margerum, Richard D. 2001.
Organizational commitment to integrated and collaborative management: matching strategies to constraints. Environmental Management. 28(4): 421-431.

Mattessich, Paul W.; Murray-Close, Marta; Monsey, Barbara R. 2001.
Collaboration: what makes it work. A review of research literature on factors influencing successful collaboration. 2d ed. St. Paul, MN: Wilder Foundation. 82 p.

McCloskey, Michael. 1996.
The skeptic: collaboration has its limits. High Country News. [Available only on Internet: http://www.hcn.org/servlets/hcn.Article?article_id=1839].

McCloskey, Michael. 1999.
Local communities and the management of public forests. Ecology Law Quarterly. 25(4): 624-629.

Mendez, S.R.; Carroll, M.S.; Blatner, K.A.; *et al.* 2003.
Smoke on the hill: a comparative study of wildfire and two communities. Western Journal of Applied Forestry. 18(1):60-70.

Mohai, P.; Jakes, P. 1996.
The Forest Service in the 1990s. Journal of Forestry. 94(1): 31-37.

Mohai, P.; Stillman, P.; Jakes, P.; Liggett, C. 1994.
Change in the USDA Forest Service: are we heading in the right direction? Gen. Tech. Rep. NC-172. St. Paul, MN: U.S. Department of Agriculture, Forest Service, North Central Forest Experiment Station. 129 p.

Moore, Elizabeth A.; Koontz, Tomas M. 2003.
A typology of collaborative watershed groups: citizen-based, agency-based, and mixed partnerships. Society and Natural Resources. 16: 451-460.

Moote, Ann. 2003.
Form and function of large scale collaborative planning processes. Flagstaff, AZ: Ecological Restoration Institute, Northern Arizona University. 10 p.

Moote, Ann; Becker, Dennis, eds. 2003.
Exploring barriers to collaborative forestry. Report from a workshop held at Hart Prairie, Flagstaff, AZ; 2003 September 17-19. Flagstaff, AZ: Ecological Restoration Institute, Northern Arizona University. 23 p.

NAPA, National Academy of Public Administration. 2003.
Resource materials for participants in Academy's Wildfire Workshops on hazard mitigation and enhanced local preparedness. Washington, DC: National Academy of Public Administration. 177 p.

NWCG, National Wildfire Coordinating Group. 1999.
Establishing fire prevention education cooperative programs and partnerships. Rep. NFES#2597. Boise, ID: National Interagency Fire Center. n.p.

Norris-York, Dover. 1996.
The Federal Advisory Committee Act: barrier or boon to effective natural resource management? Environmental Law. 26: 419-446

NRLC, Natural Resources Law Center. 1998.
The state role in western watershed initiatives. Rep.RR-18. Boulder, CO: University of Colorado, Natural Resources Law Center. 91 p.

NRLC, Natural Resources Law Center. 2000.
Laws influencing community-based conservation in Colorado and the American West: a primer. Boulder, CO: University of Colorado, Natural Resources Law Center. 51 p.

Paulson, Deborah D.; Chamberlin, Katherine M. 1998.
Guidelines and issues to consider in planning a collaborative process. Laramie, WY: Department of Geography and Recreation, University of Wyoming. 14 p. [Available only on Internet: http://www.uwyo.edu/enr/ienr/DPReport.html].

Pipkin, James; Doerksen, Harvey. 2000.
Collaboration in natural resource management: selected case studies. Washington, DC: U.S. Department of the Interior. 216 p.

Porter, Douglas R.; Salvesen, David A. 1995.
Collaborative planning for wetlands and wildlife. Washington, DC: Island Press. 293 p.

President's Council on Sustainable Development. 1997.
Lessons learned from collaborative approaches. [Available only on Internet: http://clinton4.nara.gov/PCSD/Publications/Progress_Report.html].

Propst, Luther; Rosan, Liz. 1997.
National parks and their neighbors: lessons from the field on building partnerships with local communities. Tucson, AZ: Sonoran Institute. 16 p.

Provan, Keith G.; Milward, H. Brinton. 2001.
Do networks really work? A framework for evaluating public-sector organized networks. Public Administration Review. 61(4): 414-424.

Rana, Naureen. 2002.
Final Farm Bill Recap. Washington, DC: Pinchot Institute for Conservation. [Available only on Internet: http://www.pinchot.org/pic/farmbill/recap.html].

Rickenbach, Mark G.; Reed, A. Scott. 2002.
Cross-boundary cooperation in a watershed context: the sentiments of private forest landowners. Environmental Management. 30(4): 584-594.

Rieke, Betsy. 1998.
The Federal Advisory Committee Act: impacts on community-based, collaborative groups. Forest Trust Quarterly Report. 18: 3 p.

Rolle, Su. 2002.
Measures of progress for collaboration: case study of the Applegate partnership. Gen. Tech. Rep. PNW-565. Portland, OR: U.S. Department of Agriculture, Forest Service, Pacific Northwest Research Station. 13 p.

Round Tables on the Environment and Economy in Canada. 1998.
Building consensus for a sustainable future. Ottawa, Ontario, Canada: National Round Table on the Environment and the Economy. 15 p. [Available only on Internet: http://www.mediate.com/articles/consen.cfm].

Schindler-Rainman, Eva; Lippit, Ronald. 1993.
Building collaborative communities. In: Weisbord, Marvin R., ed. Discovering common ground: how future search conferences bring people together to achieve breakthrough innovation, empowerment, shared vision and collaborative action. San Francisco, CA: Berret-Koehler: 35-43.

Schuett, Michael A.; Selin, Steven W.; Carr, Deborah S. 2001.
Making it work: keys to successful collaboration in natural resource management. Environmental Management. 27(4): 587-593.

Selin, Steven; Chavez, Deborah. 1995.
Developing a collaborative model for environmental planning and management. Environmental Management. 19(2): 189-195.

Selin, Steven; Schuett, Michael; Carr, Deborah. 1997.
Has collaborative planning taken root in the National Forests? Journal of Forestry. 95(5): 25-28.

Selin, Steven W.;
Schuett, Michael A.;
Carr, Debbie. 2000.
Modeling stakeholder perceptions of collaborative initiative effectiveness. Society and Natural Resources. 13: 735-745.

Shaffer, S.; Shipley, J.
2002.
Appligate communities' collaborative fire protection strategy: the Applegate Fire Plan. Lessons learned from our project. Applegate, OR: Applegate Partnership. On file with: U.S. Department of Agriculture, Forest Service, North Central Research Station, 1992 Folwell Ave., St. Paul, MN 55108. 14 p.

Shindler, Bruce A.;
Brunson, Mark; Stankey,
George H. 2002.
Social acceptability of forest conditions and management practices: a problem analysis. Gen. Tech. Rep. PNW-537. Portland, OR: U.S. Department of Agriculture, Forest Service, Pacific Northwest Research Station. 68 p.

Singleton, Sara. 2002.
Collaborative environmental planning in the American West: the good, the bad and the ugly. Environmental Politics. 11(3): 54-75.

Sirmon, Jeff. 2001.
Collaborative stewardship training opportunities: a report to the USDA Forest Service. Washington, DC: Pinchot Institute. n.p.

Smith, Patrick D.;
McDonough, Maureen
H. 2001. B
eyond public participation: fairness in natural resource decision making. Society and Natural Resources. 14: 239-249.

Society of American
Foresters. 2004.
Preparing a community wildfire protection plan: a handbook for wildland-urban interface communities. Washington, DC: Society of American Foresters. 11 p.

Southern Utah Wilderness
Alliance. 1994.
Why one advocacy group steers clear of consensus efforts. High Country News. [Available only on Internet: http://www.hcn.org/servlets/hcn.Article?article_id=373].

Steelman, Toddi;
Kunkel, Ginger. 2003.
Community responses to wildland fire threats in New Mexico. 2003. [Available only on Internet: http://www.ncsu.edu/project/wildfire].

Sturtevant, Victoria;
Corson, Corinne. 2003.
Applegate communities' collaborative fire protection strategy (Applegate Fire Plan): participants' thoughts about process and outcome. Ashland, OR: Southern Oregon University. 55 p.

Sturtevant, V.; Jakes, P.J.
2003.
The Applegate fire plan: steps to improve community preparedness for wildfire. Community Preparedness Case Study #3. St. Paul, MN: U.S. Department of Agriculture, Forest Service, North Central Research Station. 4 p.

Sturtevant, Victoria;
Lange, Jonathan. 1995.
Applegate partnership case study: group dynamics and community context. Ashland, OR: Southern Oregon University. On file with: U.S. Department of Agriculture, Forest Service, Pacific Northwest Research Station, 400 N. 34th St . Suite 201, Seattle, WA 98103. 103 p.

Susskind, Lawrence;
McKearnan, Sarah;
Thomas-Larmer,
Jennifer. 1999.
The consensus building handbook. Thousand Oaks, CA: Sage Publications. 1,147 p.

Sustainable Northwest;
Wallowa Resources; The
Watershed Research &
Training Center. 2002.
Working together to facilitate change. Portland, OR: Sustainable Northwest. 40 p.

SWIFT, Southwest
Interface Team. 2003.
Profile and Program or Work, C.Y. 2003-2004. 61 p.

Takahashi, Lois M.;
Smutny, Gayla. 2001.
Collaboration among small, community-based organizations: strategies and challenges in turbulent environments. Journal of Planning Education and Research. 21: 141-153.

Teie, W.C.; Weatherford,
B.F. 2000.
A report to the Council of Western State Foresters: fire in the West, the wildland/urban interface fire problem. Rescue, CA: Deer Valley Press. 80 p.

Thomas, Craig. 1999.
Linking public agencies with community-based watershed organizations: lessons from California. Policy Studies Journal. 27(3): 544-564.

TNC, The Nature Conservancy Fire Learning Network. 2003. *Improved collaboration advances implementation of fire restoration strategies.* The Nature Conservancy. [Available only on Internet: http://tnc-ecomanagement.org/images/FLN3summary.pdf].

United States Department of Agriculture, Forest Service. 1995. *Collaborative planning: sustaining forests and communities.* Rep. FS-578. Washington, DC: U.S. Department of Agriculture, Forest Service. 8 p.

United States Department of Agriculture, Forest Service. 2002. *Desk guide for contracting under existing authorities for service contracts with product removal.* On file with: U.S. Department of Agriculture, Forest Service, North Central Research Station, 1992 Folwell Avenue, St. Paul, MN 55108. 187 p.

United States Department of Agriculture, Forest Service. 2003a. *USDA Forest Service National Fire Plan Research & Development.* Misc. Pub. 1588. Washington, DC: U.S. Department of Agriculture, Forest Service. 52 p.

United States Department of Agriculture, Forest Service. 2003b. *The principle laws relating to the USDA Forest Service State and Private Forestry Programs.* FS-758. Washington, DC: U.S. Department of Agriculture, Forest Service. 52 p.

United States Department of Agriculture, Forest Service Collaborative Stewardship Team. 2000. *Collaborative stewardship within the Forest Service: findings and recommendations from the National Collaborative Stewardship Team.* 64 p.

United States Department of Agriculture and United States Department of Interior. 2000. *Managing the impact of wildfire on communities and the environment: a report to the President in response to the wildfires of 2000.* [Available only on Internet: http://www.fireplan.gov/reports/8-20-en.pdf].

United States Department of Agriculture and United States Department of Interior. 2001. *A collaborative approach for reducing wildland fire risks to communities and the environment: 10-year comprehensive strategy.* [Available only on Internet: http://www.fireplan.gov/reports/7-19-en.pdf].

United States Department of Interior, Fish and Wildlife Service. 2000. *Collaborative resource management: a pilot interagency training course.* Shepherdstown, WA: National Conservation Training Center. n.p.

United States General Accounting Office. 1991. *Designing evaluations.* Rep. GAO/PMED-10.1.4. Washington, DC: United States General Accounting Office. n.p.

United States General Accounting Office. 2003. *Program evaluation: an evaluation culture and collaborative partnerships help build agency capacity.* Rep. GAO-03-454. Washington, DC: United States General Accounting Office. 29 p.

United States Government. n.d. *Healthy Forests.* www.healthyforests.gov

University of Kansas. 2003. *Community tool box.* [Available only on Internet: http://ctb.ku.edu].

United States Department of the Interior, Bureau of Land Management, and Sonorian Institute. 2000. *A desktop reference guide to collaborative, community-based planning.* Tucson, AZ: Sonoran Institute. 20 p.

Waage, Sissel. 2003. *Collaborative salmon recovery planning: examining decision making and implementation in northeastern Oregon.* Society and Natural Resources. 16: 295-307.

Walker, G.B.; Daniels, S.E. 2001. *Natural resource policy and the paradox of public involvement: bringing scientists and citizens together.* Journal of Sustainable Forestry. 13(1/2): 253-269.

Weber, Edward P. 1999. *The question of accountability in historical perspective: from Jackson to contemporary grassroots ecosystem management.* Administration & Society. 31(4): 451-494.

Weber, Edward P. 2003.
Bringing society back in: grassroots ecosystem management, accountability, and sustainable communities. Cambridge, MA: MIT Press. 317 p.

Webler, Thomas; Tuler, Seth; Shockey, Ingrid; Stern, Paul; Beattie, Robert. 2003.
Participation by local government officials in watershed management planning. Society and Natural Resources. 16: 105-121.

White, Alan T.; Zeitlyn, Hale Lynne; Yves, Renard; Lafcadio, Cortesi, eds. 1994.
Collaborative and community-based management of Coral Reefs: lessons from experience. West Hartford, CT: Kumarian Press. 130 p.

Williams, Ellen M.; Ellefson, Paul V. 1996.
Natural resource partnerships: factors leading to cooperative success in the management of landscape level ecosystems involving mixed ownership. St. Paul, MN: University of Minnesota. 81 p.

Williams, Ellen M; Ellefson, Paul V. 1997.
Going into partnership to manage a landscape. Journal of Forestry. 95(5): 29-33.

Wondolleck, Julia M.; Yaffee, Steven L. 2000.
Making collaboration work: lessons from innovation in natural resource management. Washington, DC: Island Press. 277 p.

Yaffee, Steven L.; Phillips, Ali F.; Frentz, Irene C.; *et al.* 1996.
Ecosystem management in the United States: an assessment of current experience. Washington, DC: Island Press. 352 p.

Yaffee, Steven L.; Wondolleck, Julia M. 2000.
Making collaboration work. Conservation Biology in Practice. 1(1): 17-25.

Yaffee, Steven; Schueller, Sheila; Higgs, Stephen; Dotzour, Althea; Wondolleck, Julia. 2004.
Measuring progress: an evaluation guide for ecosystem and community-based projects. Ann Arbor, MI: Ecosystem Management Initiative, School of Natural Resources and Environment, University of Michigan. 140 p.